SCIENCE *and* ENVIRONMENT *in* VEDIC SANATAN RELIGION

VIJAY KUMAR PANDEY

notionpress.com

INDIA • SINGAPORE • MALAYSIA

ISBN 979-8-89233-429-7

Dedication

The book is dedicated to my mentor and maternal uncle, (late) Dr. Bhagirath Mishra, a renowned academician in Hindi literature, who not only achieved very high positions in academics, name and fame but also exhibited a super blend of traditions, religion, ethics and modernity, which served as a role model to me, inspiring me and many others to follow the same in life.

CONTENTS

INTRODUCTION

The manner of teaching in science has led to a misconception in the minds of some people, leading to the belief that anything which cannot be explained by any known science is irrational and orthodox. Therefore, in the name of science and modernity, some people have been deploring the Vedic Sanatan religion and its tenets and customs as being unscientific and orthodox as these cannot be explained by any known science. This is just a misconception because only when something is proved wrong by any known science can it be labeled as unscientific. But, if anything just cannot be explained by any known science, it is a matter for more detailed investigations.

Many things cannot be fully explained by the physical and biological sciences, such as emotions, opinions, wishes, willpower, urges, etc. Besides the anatomy and physiology of the brain, conscience and consciousness significantly affect the functioning of the mind, which can cause considerable differences in the perception and behavior of different persons, despite coming from similar backgrounds. Human behavior can be better understood through social sciences, which deal with the varied aspects of human thinking more vividly. Human beings are more social than other animals. Without family, friends and society, anyone would feel quite alone, like Robinson Crusoe on the virgin island. Further, natural environment is the ultimate provident for all human needs, from food, clothing and shelter to air, water, land, minerals, medicines and all kinds of energies. Therefore, the ancient Vedic theologians accorded prime importance to the preservation of both our social environment as well as the natural environment while formulating tenets, rites and socio-religious customs of the religion. Though modern science was not known in ancient times, the Vedic theologians discovered the ancient science of logic and wisdom in deciding the early model of growth and development. This helped the country not only achieve tremendous progress in both spiritual and material fields but also preserved the social milieu as well as the natural resource base for millenniums, until recent times.

Around the 20th century, the western science and technology model was adopted in the country for faster materialistic growth. Since then, materialistic growth has been occurring quite fast. However, this has also led to faster degradation in the natural resource base and social ambiance. In the pretext of scientific and modern living, religion and socio-religious customs are now being labeled as unscientific and orthodox. This is a misconception that is reducing religious fervor, which till recently helped in preserving the social environment as well as the natural environment, both of which are now deteriorating very fast. Therefore, it is considered worthwhile to examine the scientific connotations as well as the environmental concerns in the tenets, rites and socio-religious customs of the Vedic Sanatan religion.

The present book attempts this examination. The search for scientific connotations in the tenets and customs of the religion is based on simple senior school-level science to make it easily understandable to the people, especially the younger generation. Environmental concerns are searched through the elemental wisdom underlying these tenets and customs, which have helped preserve the social milieu and/or the natural resource base. The book finds that most of the tenets and rites of the religion and socio-religious customs do contain some scientific connotations or have some elemental wisdom that helps preserve the social milieu and/or the natural resource base. Only one tenet, describing the soul's travel to the invisible world after death, does not seem to have any scientific connotation, and this tenet can be easily discarded without any loss in religious intent, practice and fervor. A few socio-religious customs are recently being followed in an orthodox manner due to the new admix of current technology, which if removed, can make these customs more pious, full of wisdom and rationality as suggested in the text. Therefore, all those who deeply care for the social ambiance and natural environment must follow the Vedic Sanatan religion, its tenets, rites and socio-religious customs with full enthusiasm and pride for being fully scientific and/or full of wisdom for preserving the social ambiance and natural environment.

The present book, however, does not intend to provide a full treatise on the Vedic Sanatan religion. It only summarizes the tenets, rites and customs of the religion, devoting more space to search therein for the scientific connotations and/or the elemental wisdom for preserving the environment—which is the main task of the present book. These tenets, rites and customs have been drawn, adapted and summarized exclusively from the book "SANATAN DHARMA, an elementary textbook of HINDU RELIGION AND ETHICS" published by the Board of Trustees, Central Hindu College (now Benares Hindu University), Benares in 1916, and digitized for the

Microsoft Corporation in 2007. This book, compiled by scholars, presents a full treatise on "SANATAN DHARMA" in English along with respective Sanskrit shlokas and their explanations, and is available both online and in print for more curious readers.

Gratefully acknowledge the comments and suggestions on the earlier draft of the present book from Dr. S. K. Tiwari, a retired professor.

Vijay Kumar Pandey
RH A2, Sunshree Emerald RH Co-Op. Housing Society,
N.I.B.M. Road, Kondhwa,
PUNE - 411048.
Email ID: vkpandey1941@gmail.com

CHAPTER

RELIGION, SCIENCE AND ENVIRONMENT 01

1.1 EVOLUTION OF RELIGION

According to science, about 13.5 billion years ago, the BIG BANG (great explosion) occurred, which led to the formation of energy, matter, time and space. The planet Earth was formed about 4.5 billion years ago, on which an emergence of organisms occurred about 3.8 billion years ago. The evolution of the genus Homo took place about 2.5 million years ago in Africa, and in due course of time, moved from Africa to Eurasia about 2 million years ago. Thereafter, different human species were evolved, e.g., Homo erectus, Neanderthals, Homo sapiens, etc. The Homo sapiens evolved about 200,000 years ago. In the early periods of human evolution, all human species were foragers who fed themselves by gathering plants and hunting animals in jungles. Over the years, only the Sapiens survived while the other species vanished. About 10,000 years ago, the Sapiens began to devote almost all their time and effort to manipulating the lives of a few animal and plant species. It was a revolution in the way humans lived—the Agricultural Revolution (Yuval Noah Harari, 2014, P.87). This revolution led to a great deal of subsequent developments in human history.

The advent of agriculture led to the concept of group living and village community as a unit for safety, security and cultural development. The progress in agriculture liberated the human mind from the botherations of hunger and food. The human mind then started venturing into other areas of creativity and productivity, such as communication (language and script development, literature writing, etc.), habitation and construction, textiles, mining and metallurgy, music, fine arts and philosophy. The historical monuments and archaic findings, including manuscripts of ancient writings, are a testimony to ancient creativity and productivity. Archaic excavations in Egypt, Greece, Mesopotamia (West Asia), India, China and South America have discovered the existence of developed ancient civilizations dated around 2000 BCE and even earlier. The findings of these archaic excavations exhibit fairly high levels of ancient developments in agriculture, textiles, medical care, town planning and the existence of cities, kingdoms ruled by various kings, script development and writings, mining and metallurgy – especially of iron and copper for tools and house wares, dance and music, paintings and sculptures, etc. These human minds ventured into creativity and productivity, which led to greater and closer interactions of humans with the various elements of nature and its various phenomena while undertaking travels to different places in search of new materials and knowledge. These travels served to provide a great deal of knowledge and wisdom to human beings in evolving and shaping their living and creativity.

During their travels to far-off places, humans encountered different elements of nature such as land terrains and soils, ponds, lakes and rivers, rainfall patterns, temperature variations, forests, plants and trees, other human beings, animals and other living species. This experience revealed great diversity in the various elements of nature in terms of size, shape, color, pattern and behavior among different types of plants, trees, animals, birds and aquatic life. Even among the inanimate materials like soils, rocks, pebbles, etc., big diversity was observed in terms of texture, hardness and constituent components. This experience also revealed orderliness and self-regulation in nature's various phenomena like cycles of temperature variations and rainfall patterns during a year, regeneration of local flora and fauna, seasonal reproduction of flowers and fruits, etc. It was also observed that there existed some remarkable interdependence among the different elements of nature, wherein plants and trees depend on living beings, who in turn depend on plants and trees. This showed some symbiotic relationship of interdependence between them.

Observations were made about the different processes of regeneration and degeneration of life through birth, growth and death cycles. These seemed to appear in quite a regular, orderly and self-regulating manner in different living beings, ranging from micro-size organisms to jumbo-size animals, as well as from aquatic to land-based living beings. They all were found to be very amazing to human curiosity. Similarly, orderliness and self-regulation of weather cycles (summer, rain and winter), and then the dynamic cycle of the movement of the sun, moon and other planets were found to be quite amazing. The interdependence of all these cycles and their impact on the providences of nature (such as air, water, food, fiber, fuel and other materials), affecting the life of all living creatures were found to be not only quite astonishing but also gratuitous. They discovered that without these providences from nature, their own living as that of other living beings, was impossible. Catastrophes like floods, droughts, storms, etc., were also observed. All these myriad observations and revelations about nature and its various phenomena bewildered the human mind. It generated an obvious curiosity in human minds about the source, regulation and control of all nature's creation.

After deep pondering, the human minds conceived the existence of some supernatural power that creates, regulates and controls different elements of nature and their various phenomena. In addition, they perceived this supernatural power as being very caring to all living beings for their sustenance and living by providing food, air, water and other materials through various providences of nature. At times, they also perceived this supernatural power as being quite punishing through its wrath by way of excess rain, flood or drought, etc. They then bestowed their full faith in this supernatural power and started revering and worshiping it for its benevolence. This belief and faith in the supernatural power led to the evolution of religion in different ancient civilizations. This was an excellent intellectual creativity of the human minds, which became a dogma all over the world—although in varied forms—giving rise to several different religions in different ancient civilizations. The advent of religion not only gave solace and peace to the anxious and curious human mind, but also made it a gratuitous community of citizens, believing and practicing the specific religious dogmas in different civilizations. Religion has also proved to be the best cohesive and moral force among its believers in all civilizations through time immemorial. These beneficial aspects of religion were realized by all civilizations across the world, which led to its practice through all ages.

With a growth in population and other developments in lifestyle, community living expanded from villages to cities, which posed new problems of security, law and order and social cohesion. These issues were not faced much in the earlier tribal communities that lived a primitive life and were governed by their tribal kings. Advancements in civilization led to a development in intellectual pursuits, habitation and construction, industry, trade and commerce, civil administration, etc. All these developments generated corresponding social and cultural complexities arising due to self-esteem and pride among different groups of people having different statuses and achievement levels. This often led to clashes and wars of nerve among them, disturbing social cohesion in group living. The conception of a supernatural power and its reverence and worship as a religion served both purposes: first, to comfort the human mind that was curious about the source of all creation in nature and the universe, and second, to infuse a sense of social cohesion and compassion among the people in group living, along with a moral fear of the wrath of the supernatural power in case of immoral and antisocial conduct. All this worked quite well for several millenniums, witnessing growth and development in various fields all over the world.

1.2 RELIGIOUS MYTHOLOGIES AND CUSTOMS

Most of the religions comprise three components. The first component is faith and trust in a supernatural power as the creator and governor of the universe; the second component is the form of the supernatural power, religious tenets and rites, method of reverence and worship developed as DHARMA or duty to be followed by the believers; and the third component is a set of socio-religious customs that evolved as a part of the way of life for virtuous and harmonious living. On the first component of faith and trust, there is virtually no difference among most of the religions of the world. Only the name or the word used to address the supernatural power is different, such as ISHWARA, ALLAH, GOD, etc. Though explained in different words of different languages in the ancient scriptures of different religions, most of the religions primarily believe in a formless, invisible supernatural power that is infinite, with no beginning and no end. It governs the entire universe through its own mechanics. It is difficult to comprehend such a supernatural power through the five senses or even the most developed super-mind of a human being. It can only be conceptualized and realized. All this conceptualization connotes the real meaning of religion in a true sense, i.e., the conception of a supernatural power as a matter of belief, faith and trust, which is the same in all religions. For over several millenniums, this belief served to resolve the curiosities of mankind about the creation and governance of nature and the universe, as also to provide a forum for union, cohesion and compassion among the believers of a specific religion.

The second component comprises the form of the supernatural power, its tenets and rites as well as the method of reverence and worship, which differ widely among various religions. In all religions, the supernatural power connects with its believers through various messengers—known differently in different religions—such as RISHIS, PAIGAMBER, MESSIAH, etc. They guide their believers through their especial performances, sermons and writings about belief in a particular form of the supernatural power, tenets and rites of the religion and method of expressing reverence to it. This linkage of the supernatural power through these messengers is quite different in various religions of the world. The stories of these messengers, their messages, form of the supernatural power, incarnations or other associated apostles and acclaimed religious luminaries are described in the holy religious scriptures of different religions. In addition, most religions also contain some supernatural elements and mystical concepts of divine nature that are also described in the ancient scriptures. All such stories about the messengers and their guidance, holy books containing tenets and rites, supernatural events and mystical concepts constitute the mythologies of different religions inherited over the millenniums and mislabeled as different religions. However, in common parlance, people believe in these mythologies as a part of their religion with complete faith and trust. This book also uses the term religion as prevalent in the common parlance, i.e., including faith and trust as well as the mythologies.

To illustrate further, the messengers and forms of representation of the supernatural power in three main religions are as follows. In the Vedic Sanatan religion, the supernatural power is called BRAHMAN or ISHWARA, who is formless and revealed to ancient RISHIS as His messengers who wrote the holy scriptures, the Vedas, as revelations from BRAHMAN. The BRAHMAN is formless, but for comprehension of the common people, it is also revealed as a visual trinity called BRAHMA, VISHNU and SHIVA, which are called BHAGWANS to differentiate them from BRAHMAN. In the Islam religion, the supernatural power is called ALLAH, who is formless and revealed to Prophet MOHAMMED as His messenger who wrote the holy Koran as the revelations from ALLAH. In the Christian religion, the supernatural power is called GOD, who is formless and revealed to Messiah JESUS CHRIST as His messenger whose teachings of the new testaments along with other ancient writings comprised the Bible, their holy book. Thus, BRAHMAN, ALLAH and GOD are all formless and are differently revealed to different messengers in these three religions. The messengers and their revelations, the forms of representation of the supernatural power, the holy books containing tenets and rites as well as some supernatural events and mystical religious concepts constitute the religious mythologies of these three religions. These mythologies differ widely among the religions. In fact, there is no area of similarity among the mythologies of these religions for any comparison. It is only an expression of unnecessary superiority that often leads to comparison and conflict among the believers of these religions. But this superiority complex is an antithesis to the very concept of religion, which is only an expression of belief, faith and trust in a formless, invisible and infinite supernatural power, which is only named differently in different religions.

The third component is a set of socio-religious customs, which were developed with an orientation towards both religion as well as social culture. These constituted a part of the way of life of the people of a specific religion. These socio-religious customs contain an admix of some religious rites in socio-cultural practices that were developed in the ancient times. These socio-religious customs were bound to be different in different religions because of several local geophysical conditions that varied in quite extremes, such as very low temperatures in the European highlands to very high temperatures in the deserts of mid-Asia to only moderate temperatures in the plains of south-Asia. These variations in geophysical conditions largely caused differences in movements and living patterns, mode of social interactions and worship rituals. The climate, especially day and night temperatures, availability of water, land terrains, etc., significantly influenced the way of conducting daily and other routine ceremonies, and thereby the customs and rites of different religions.

The religious mythologies can be categorized into two groups: one group containing the religious tenets and rites, worship rituals and socio-religious customs, and the other group containing various religious stories about the acts of messengers, various incarnations and apostles, performances of religious luminaries and occurrences of supernatural events. Mythologies of the first group deal with the religious beliefs and practices for reverence and worship of the supernatural power as well as the conduct of some socio-religious ceremonies, often called as DHARMA or duty of the believers of the specific religion. These beliefs, practices and customs implicitly contain some underlying philosophical base that was developed by the ancient theologians as per the geophysical and social conditions prevalent in those times. The second group of mythologies relating to various religious stories deals with the narration of the acts of the various deities and ancient religious luminaries, showing either heroic performances as role models to motivate the people or as unworthy evil performances to desist people from adoption in actual life. There are also some stories of mystifying happenings in society or nature to convey some sense of divinity. The stories might have been real or just fictional, but they convey some morale and/or wisdom to the people to follow in life. Such stories are not only interesting and absorbing but are also easy to remember and serve to provide guidance in actual life. Therefore, since ages, these stories have been recognized as the most effective media for easy communication to the general people. Mythologies relating to religious stories in the Vedic Sanatan religion are very vast in number (see Pattanaik Devdatta, 2006) and require a separate space. These are not covered in the present book, which only examines the elements of scientific content and/or environmental wisdom as embodied in the tenets, rites and customs of the religion.

1.3 RELIGION AND SCIENCE

The religion mentioned now onwards in this book refers to the Vedic Sanatan religion as enumerated by the ancient rishis in the scriptures of the Vedas around 2000 BCE or even earlier. The religion has belief, faith and trust in the supernatural power called BRAHMAN or ISHWARA, which is formless, infinite and present everywhere in everything at all times, hence considered universal consciousness. The religion advocates some tenets, rites and customs to be followed as DHARMA (duty), which were conceived and developed by the ancient rishis after conducting detailed studies of various elements of and happenings in nature and society to encompass environmental concerns. Modern science is a more recent development, largely spanning over the past three centuries – the 18th, 19th and 20th centuries. Science refers to a body of knowledge obtained through systematic and methodological studies of various cause-and-effect relationships that operate in the elements of and happenings in nature and the universe. Thus, religion and science both have had a common objective of understanding nature and the universe, and evolving methods and techniques for the use of this knowledge for the betterment of mankind. Therefore, in terms of the main objective, there is not much difference between religion and science. However, the methodologies employed as also the language for presentation of the results are quite different in religion and science.

Religion generally employed an inductive approach by using the observed data on the events/ happenings in nature and society, building postulates and doing deep meditation. This led to intuitive judgments on alternate postulates and helped draw concluding inferences through an intuitive voice. In deep meditation, one is completely detached from the surroundings and the self, becomes completely thoughtless on mundane matters and gets transcendentally attached to universal consciousness. In deep meditation, one gets intuition, which is a truthful revelation on any issue that is free of all mundane biases and reasoning. Thus, intuition is an inner voice, a power of knowing something without conscious reasoning. All the knowledge contained in the ancient scriptures of the Vedas was an intuitive revelation as a message from the supernatural power of BRAHMAN. The intuitive revelation on any specific postulate was made to some ancient rishi and was later discussed amongst the other ancient rishis through SHASTRARTHA (religious discussion). After receiving the consensus from the group of rishis, the revelation was accepted as an inference for inclusion into the ancient scriptures. Thus, the ancient scriptures of the Vedas were based on revelations made to several rishis, duly consented to by other rishis through religious discussions.

Science employed a deductive approach by first using the observed data of the happenings in nature for the simulation and representation of the same happenings in well-planned experiments conducted in a laboratory or field. Then, the experiment was replicated several times and the data in each replication was collected. Thus, the data collected through science experiments is more numerically measured and verifiable. Thereafter, analysis of the experimental data is done to discover laws and axioms operating therein, drawing concluding inferences from the results of the experiments. The results of the experiment are then made public through seminars or publications in scientific journals for obtaining views, comments and even contradictions from other scientists. Once verified by other scientists, the law and inference drawn becomes a scientific theory. Thus, science is more procedural and verifiable. It is for this reason that the application of science is generally sought in judging the veracity of any concept or happening. However, since science deals with only physical phenomena, the above criteria can more truly be applied only for testing the veracity of a physical phenomenon. Therefore, the knowledge of science will be quite inappropriate for testing the veracity of a metaphysical and abstract phenomenon.

In fact, both religion and science are the inquisitive disciplines of the human mind and intelligence. The objectives of both are the same, i.e., to understand nature and the universe, and use this knowledge for the betterment of humanity. But their approaches are different. Science deals with the physical aspect of knowledge through experimentation, while religion deals with the metaphysical aspect of knowledge through meditation. However, both reached an almost similar ultimate conclusion, though stated in different words of different languages. Modern science, as known in the common parlance, comprises two broad fields of physical sciences and biological sciences. The mission of physical sciences has been to study matter and find the ultimate constituent of the universe. The mission of biological sciences has been to study the creation of life and its constituents. The mission of religion has been to discover the supernatural power and its mechanics in regulating nature and the universe.

Modern physical science studied the physical properties of matter in terms of mass and electric charge to discover the ultimate constituent or building block of the universe. Initially, an atom was conceived as the smallest unit of matter. But later, studies discovered that an atom comprises even smaller sub-atomic particles – electrons, protons and neutrons. Further studies discovered a large variety of puzzling finer sub-atomic particles, such as different types of electrons, quarks and neutrinos that revolve inside an atom. More recent experiments conducted through the LARGE HADRON COLLIDER (LHC) in 2012 and onwards found different types of sub-atomic particles that were all massless and revolved in their respective energy fields, which when excited provided mass to the respective particle. Then the attention shifted from atomic particles to the energy fields that operate inside an atom. There were already some earlier known energy fields like the electro-magnetic field, weak nuclear field and strong nuclear field. So, energy fields were considered as the building blocks of matter and the universe. All these fields were found to be closely entangled and interacting with each other as waves of energy quanta, which gave rise to the concept of the Quantum Fields of Energy, pervading through all of space in the universe. However, scientists were unable to measure the quantum fields due to it being multidimensional in nature as "ripples of waves of fluid-like substance continuously bubbling, vibrating and oscillating energy quantum" (David Tong, 2017). Some physicists described quantum fields innately nonmaterial in nature (Mani Bhaumic, 2021). However, most other physicists did not notice this, possibly due to their sole concern being the physical matter and its constituents.

The observation made by some physicists about the quantum fields being nonmaterial in nature seems to have a valid substance. The "ripples of waves of fluid-like substance continuously bubbling, vibrating and oscillating energy quantum" indicate pulsation in the quantum fields. Pulsation is the characteristic feature of a living force. It is this pulsation that differentiates between inert matter and living force. Inert matter is a physical entity perceptible through the human senses and occupies a fixed space as determined by its physical properties such as mass, size, form, electric charge, etc. However, the living force of consciousness is not perceptible by the human senses as it does not occupy a fixed space. Instead, it is all-pervading in space and can only be realized through its impulse for creativity. The pulsation indicates the presence of a living force of consciousness with a creative urge in the quantum field. Without this creative urge of consciousness, the universe would have just been an inert floating mass of hot gaseous floats and/or cooled-down solid rocks after the BIG BANG explosion. It is this pulsation of conscious creative urge that has created so much diversity in the universe and multiverse, and is still leading these to expand further. It is this conscious creative urge that regulates and controls the quantum energy fields to lay mass to massless subatomic particles. This laying of mass is done not equally to all the particles but in a discretionary manner that adds more mass to some particles and less mass to others, while some remain without any mass. It is this conscious creative urge that creates not just matter but different types of matter leading to 118 elements in the periodic table of elements. All these observations represent some sort of living discretionary power, which substantiates the presence of live force as a consciousness with a creative urge in the quantum fields.

The religion believes in the presence of both living energy and material energy in the universe. In metaphysics, BRAHMAN is conceived as being both the material energy and the spirit, which is the live energy of a creative urge called universal consciousness. The ancient Vedic rishis had conceived BRAHMAN as an infinite, formless and 'all-pervading' supernatural power, manifesting itself in a subtle form called JIVA into all nonliving as well as living beings. To what else this conception of BRAHMAN could refer other than the infinite formless energy source whose subtle quanta is present in all living beings and inert matters? Only energy can be conceived to be formless, infinite and present everywhere and in everything. No other conceptualization could encompass all three characteristics of BRAHMAN—formless, infinite and all-pervading—except the grand energy source. Therefore, the concept of BRAHMAN, as conceived in the religion, is quite similar to the concept of the quantum energy fields, which is also formless, infinite and present everywhere in the universe, as recently discovered in physical science. Only the language used in the descriptions, e.g., Sanskrit for BRAHMAN in religion and English for quantum energy fields in science, are different. Thus, physical science and religion both converge together on the existence of a formless, infinite energy as the constituent of everything in this universe, except that physical science considers only material energy as the constituent, whereas religion considers both material and nonmaterial living forms of energy as the constituents of the universe. In religion, this living energy is regarded as the Super Consciousness, which feels, thinks and observes even in its subtle form and regulates the material energy to take certain forms under specific prevalent conditions.

The concept of super consciousness has also been explained through BELL's theorem of modern science, which implies that any change or happening at any point in the universe will cause an instantaneous change in the condition at some other point in the universe, irrespective of the distance between these points (Mathur P.C., 2016, P.11). This theorem was propounded in 1964 by John S. Bell, a renowned physicist, and was experimentally proven in 1972 by other physicists. The instantaneous transfer of signals between two points in the universe indicates the presence of eternal continuity to act as the medium of transfer. In some inexplicable manner, apparently, separate forms of matter or energy are connected to each other in the universe through this medium. This is known as an entanglement between the two particles that are far off in space, and has been scientifically proven by the three physics Nobel Laureates of 2022, viz., Alain Aspect, Anton Zellinger and John Clauser. Scientists are wondering about the medium and speed of signal transfers, which seem perhaps to be more than the speed of light. The ancient sages had envisaged the super consciousness of the supreme as pervading throughout the universe, leaving no void. This super consciousness acts as the medium for such transfers of signals (Mathur P.C., 2016, P.13).

Modern biological science studied the finer details of a living cell and developed a stem cell into a fully grown animal—a sheep. But it has not been able to create a living cell or conclusively demonstrate how life is created in a living cell. The theory of evolution, as enunciated by Charles Darwin and generally accepted, begins after the creation of a living cell. Some scientists have succeeded in synthesizing the requisite amino acids and a DNA-like structure in the laboratory, but the synthesized structure did not replicate to become a living cell. Some scientists now postulate that life was created through a chance chemical reaction in an abiogenesis process, billions of years ago. According to them, the basic constituents of a living cell, the amino acids, were produced through a chance chemical reaction in some pond of water, under favorable conditions. Then, some of these newly formed amino acids further combined together again by some chance and formed the DNA of simple structured bacteria cells. Such simple structured cells later led to further reproduction of more complex structured living cells and gradually to other life forms through replication, mutation and the natural selection processes over billions of years since the formation of the earth.

In fact, for cell formation and replication, DNA alone is not sufficient. As already stated above, DNA synthesized by some scientists in the laboratory did not replicate. Complete cellular structure, with a facilitating platform that contains plasma, protein food, mitochondrion and several other elements is required to enable cell expansion, growth and division for replication. The replication involves the mitosis process in which the division of cell nuclei containing chromosomes takes place into two exactly duplicate nuclei, each containing a similar set of chromosomes. Then the original cell divides into two cells, each containing nuclei thus produced by the division. The mitosis process is a life-generating process, a characteristic feature of growth of all living organisms. Therefore, the material energy of DNA needs to be activated by some living energy to start the life-generating process of mitosis. The chemical reaction in the water pond could have produced amino acids and DNA as material energy because only that was available in the water pond. Then what caused and activated the so-formed DNA to start the life-generating process of mitosis for cell replication? How was the complete cellular structure created and activated into living energy, leading to mitosis and cell division in the water pond? The newly propagated abiogenesis process is not clear on these accounts. Therefore, the abiogenesis process propounded for life creation appears to be simply a postulation. Further, the metamorphosis through genetic mutation and natural selection processes can lead to further growth of different varieties within any particular specie. But growth in reproduction across various diverse species under different classes, families and genera of animal and plant kingdoms needs some sort of genetic engineering in the bacteria cells for the creation of the basic elements of sexual reproduction, i.e., formation of separate male and female gametes cells and their union, leading to zygote cells in the onward sexual reproduction. How did all this genetic engineering happen in bacterial cells leading to further metamorphosis into million types of complex cells? Therefore, this abiogenesis process is just a postulation without any substantive proof through paleontological studies, i.e., fossils studies.

The religion conveys that creation of life is an act of BRAHMAN. The ancient rishis had conceptualized BRAHMAN not just as matter but also as spirit, the most powerful living force. It is this creative living force, pervading the universe, which is recognized as universal consciousness. This living force is present everywhere, in everything, in a subtle form as ANSHAH of BRAHMAN, and they called it JIVA. This JIVA, comprising both material energy and living energy as subtle consciousness, transforms itself into a living organism exhibiting a life pattern as and when some exclusively favorable ambiance is available. Of course, this concept of the ancient rishis is also a postulation without any material proof. But the observance of some nonmaterial element along with material energy in the quantum field experiment, as mentioned earlier, does give credence to the ancient rishis' concept of JIVA being both material as well as living energy. This JIVA as a subtle living energy helps the formation of living cells and creation of life.

JIVA becomes a pulsating psychosomatic matter: psycho due to the presence of consciousness as a creative urge and somatic due to the living cell it becomes in the presence of a favorable climatic environment. Modern science concepts of DNA and RNA were not known to ancient rishis. Nevertheless, they understood that JIVA could lead to the creation of life only when some specific favorable climatic conditions, as the prerequisite, were available for life creation. Modern science now explains that some amino acids and DNA could be produced under such favorable climatic conditions. Thus, a combination of the ancient thought of JIVA and the modern science thought of DNA helps understand the creation of life on earth in the presence of those specific favorable climatic conditions. When this living energy, JIVA, interacts with the DNA produced in a favorable climate, it then forms a complete cellular structure that leads to mitosis and cell replication and, thereby life begins. This is how the newly formed DNA, produced by chance, as postulated in the abiogenesis process mentioned above, might have been activated by JIVA, leading to bacterial cell formation and the beginning of life on earth. In the subsequent periods, after a billion years, when a great diversity of plants and animal species was developed, the material energy of DNA that was already present in the minuscule spores of micro-organisms, plant/tree seeds, and animal/human embryos served for a continuous flow of life creation through interaction with JIVA. Thus, the religion's concept of JIVA along with the modern science concept of DNA does help in fully understanding the life creation process. JIVA being a subtle part of BRAHMAN, the religion conveys to the common people in simple terms that life is created by BRAHMAN/ ISHWARA.

The emergence of different types of asexual and sexual regeneration could be explained through the creation of different varieties of DNA structures and consequently, different types of living cells. In different geophysical and climatic conditions, different combinations of amino acids causing varieties of DNA structures and the consequent varieties of living cell formations might have occurred. Thus, in the initial stages, billions of years earlier, different types of living cells, separately for various classes of plant and animal kingdoms, might have been formed in different time periods in different geophysical regions of the world such as in different altitudes, terrains, temperatures, and moisture levels, etc. Paleontologists have found fossils of different species of plants and animals in different agro-climatic and geophysical locations. Even today, all species of plants and animals do not naturally exist everywhere in the world. Later, migrations on account of several factors, e.g., search for better foods, protection of self from others and/or odds of nature, etc., might have led to their regional transmigrations. Thus, the religion's concept of JIVA and the modern science concept of DNA together complete the process of creation of life. Though stated in different words and languages, these thoughts of the religion and modern science are complementary to each other in explaining the creation of life on earth. Therefore, science and religion are not at crossroads, rather they provide support to each other's thoughts, though their methodologies and language of expression are quite different.

1.4 ENVIRONMENTAL CONCERNS

In order to appreciate the environmental concerns in the Vedic Sanatan religion, one should keep in mind the social philosophy of egalitarianism, i.e., equality for all with minimum inequality, as well as the developmental philosophy of sustainability, which means maintainable over time. In the very long run, spanning over a millennium, social order is maintainable only if the social environment is cohesive and inequalities in living are minimal. This is more easily possible in the case of simple living, which has minimum inequality and is more egalitarian. Luxurious living has very high inequality and loose cohesion, and therefore, is more prone to social instability and disorder in the long run. Modern-day luxurious living in some parts of the present-day world is a testimony to this, wherein social institutions of family, culture and religion are virtually disappearing, and people are unnecessarily engaged in a blatant display of superiority over others. Similarly, in the very long run, spanning over a millennium, growth and development are sustainable only if the natural resource base (e.g., land mass, water bodies, air, minerals, forests, etc.) is preserved and the phenomena of nature (e.g., rain, sunshine, climatic conditions, etc.) governing the ecosystem are not disturbed. This is possible only if the science and technology of growth and development are evolved and deployed in harmony with nature. The destructions of some ancient civilizations (e.g., MAYA culture of Latin America, Mesopotamia and Babylonia of South West Asia, etc.) by the wrath of nature are a testimony of unstable growth and development due to the over-exploitation of natural resources. Even in present times, the growth and development generated through modern science and technology in many countries of the world are now becoming unsustainable because they are leading to severe air and water pollution, health hazards, destruction of the natural resource base and drastic climate changes. These are all signs indicative of the wrath of nature due to its over-exploitation.

In fact, there is one very big difference between the vision of modern science and that of the religion. The discoveries of modern science largely have a commercial overtone. This is mainly because most of the discoveries of modern science are being largely financed by either taxpayers' money or industrial houses. It was so in the past to give a push to the momentum of the industrial revolution, which was underway in Europe and America in the 18th, 19th and 20th centuries. This trend is still continuing in the present times, even more vigorously and now in all the countries, to give a push to the national economic growth rate and corporate profits. Thus, the vision of modern science has been simply discovering some unknowns to facilitate some technological development, mainly for achieving economic and commercial objectives. Hence, the discoveries of modern science and the follow-up technological innovations did not care about their impact on the natural and social environment. The resultant euphoria, charm and glamour of new discoveries and their impact on comfort and luxury in living has made almost everyone overjoyed and hypnotized. In fact, modern science and technology together have often been propagated as a victory over nature. It was much later, after about three centuries, when the signs of the resultant environmental degradation and social degeneration became visible that some awareness and concern about these adverse impacts were being raised. Still, people at large are more fancied with comfort and luxury in living than mitigating these adverse environmental impacts.

Contrary to the approach of active and aggressive growth and development for luxurious living, the ancient theologian rishis consciously followed the path of natural non-resisting passive growth and development, and advocated simple living for two very important reasons. They realized that nature is the only source of all the material and energy required for growth and development. So, they thought that natural growth and development would be non-resisting from nature and more sustainable. They had realized, rather apprehended, that if nature is unduly exploited it might create some catastrophic conditions for resisting and inhibiting further growth and development. Therefore, the first and foremost reason was their utmost concern to work in harmony with nature instead of conquering it. The second most important reason was their equally strong concern for developing a compassionate, cohesive and egalitarian social structure because they knew that man is a more social animal and would be better governed by the social mores and taboos. They realized that family and social relations would provide a great deal of moral security and support, and also guide the human endeavor and zeal towards a more desirable path in growth and development. So, the ancient theologians devised the tenets and customs as DHARMA (duty) in the religion to protect both nature and society.

The life of human beings is influenced by two distinct environments, viz., natural environment and social environment. Natural environment relates to the various elements and phenomena of nature that construct the ecosystem, influencing the life of humans as well as that of other living beings. Social environment relates to the socio-economic structure in the society, such as state policy, public administration, leadership, family, friends, and culture (beliefs, customs and traditions), all of which guide and govern the performance of an individual as well as that of the society in terms of law and order, cohesion, creative and productive ventures. Without a social environment, an individual will just feel alone, like Robinson Crusoe on the virgin island. Therefore, the vision of the religion encompasses the preservation of both the social environment and the natural environment. So, the ancient theologians synthesized together the then-discovered knowledge of social sciences and the ecosystem in nature while enunciating tenets, rites and customs of the Vedic

Sanatan religion. Thus, the religious tenets, rites and customs encompass concerns for both the social environment and natural environment. The religious tenets and rites were evolved by the ancient rishis themselves while living an ascetic life but had great vision and concern for both society and nature.

To illustrate the social concern, after conceptualization of the NIRGUN BRAHMAN (formless ISHWARA), the sages realized that this concept would fall beyond the psychic perception of general human beings whose basic interest was more on selfish mundane matters and not on theology. So, they conceived the religion as a way of life for the general people and conceptualized SAGUN BRAHMAN (SAKAR ISHWARA) as an avatar revelation of NIRGUN BRAHMAN without bothering about the theological contradiction in it. Then it served the purpose and people got busy worshipping the various avatars of ISHWARA called BHAGWANS for everything in their life (see sub-section 2.2.2 for more details). Similarly, it was observed that a prayer conducted for some seriously ailing patient (mental or pathogenic) helped in a faster recovery. So, prayers were advocated, which later became a general practice in the religion. More often than not, prayer provides people in distress some ray of hope that ISHWARA will help and mitigate their misery. This hope rejuvenates the dispirited person and distracts him/her from other undesirable situations like depression, suicide attempt or running away.

In recent times, the cases of depression, suicide attempts, running away and antisocial acts have increased because of the subdued temperament of the religion. There is an increasing disbelief in the power of ISHWARA due to a smearing campaign led by some scientists and rationalists that describe ISHWARA and the religion as unscientific and orthodox. Science does not provide hope and peace to people in miserable conditions; rather it distracts people from ISHWARA for want of any material proof of HIS existence. But the religion does provide solace and hope to people, and this rejuvenates them to face life as it unfolds. Thus, religion has a great significance and role in maintaining social psyche and harmony among the people. Therefore, religion has been made an acceptable and feasible proposition for the masses for actual practice in life. This was often considered as a divergence from pure philosophy and theology of the formless ISHWARA by some theologians, but the divergence was accepted as wisdom in the larger interest of preserving the society as a cohesive unit (see sub-section 2.2.2 for more details). The religion, in fact, holds greater significance to the people in general than to theologians because it is the people who face the realities of a mundane life and need solace and peace in times of grief and distress. In modern times, in some societies where the fervor of religion has greatly decreased, people now have to search for consultations from some psychiatrist or mentor for their mental distress. This involves a lot of money as well as considerable running around. In traditional living, religious prayers and family care helped preserve the mental poise of a distressed person.

Similarly, protection of the natural environment was also of utmost concern when devising tenets, rites and customs of the religion for general practice. For example, trees and rivers are worshiped in the religion; this aims to create a psyche of reverence for trees and rivers among the people. This helped protect these very important components of the natural environment in the past. Such a vision is totally missing in modern science. These rituals of tree and river worship served as the most potent way of creating social awareness and action on this very important issue of preserving the natural resource base. This worked very well until recently, when both these rituals got dubbed as unscientific, backward and orthodox. The result is now quite visible in terms of forest degradation, air pollution, water pollution and wastage. Sections 3.2.1 and 4.1 delve more elaborately into this with several illustrations showing the religion's concern for protecting nature.

Thus, the vision of the religion is far different from the vision of science. Science is solely confined to either seeking more knowledge on any issue under investigation for academic purposes or developing technology for comfort and luxury in life, which ultimately leads to economic growth and/or business profit. The religion, besides metaphysical and economic pursuits, also visualized the preservation of both natural resources and social milieu for a sustainable living in the very long run not only for the benefit of mankind but also for other living beings of a lesser order. The progress on both these environmental fronts as well as metaphysical concepts and growth in economic levels of the country for more than two millenniums, until the medieval and present period, is testimony to this vision of the religion and ancient theologians. Further, the recent observations of degradation on both these fronts of social environment and natural environment due to neglect of the religion in recent times, validate the serious thoughtful environmental concern in the religion for both society and nature.

1.5 MISCONCEPTIONS ABOUT THE RELIGION

The manner of teaching in modern science has generated a temperament of science versus non-science, which attempts to portray ISHWARA, religion and its rites as unscientific orthodox concepts. This is a misconception flooding some minds that are pretending to be modern and rational. They argue that the developments in modern science have shown that the creation and governance of nature and the universe are not due to any supernatural power. They contend that there are some scientifically operating natural laws, which govern nature and the universe. They also assert the nonexistence of any scientific and material proof of the supernatural power or ISHWARA. Hence, the modernists and rationalists declare the religion and its associated practices as backward and orthodox. As a result, the two groups—one of the present-time religious saints and priests defending the religion, and second of modernists and rationalists criticizing the religion—are at loggerheads with each other on the veracity of the existence of the supernatural power and rationality of the religious rituals and customs. The kind of arguments and counter-arguments given by both these groups are misdirecting the people, especially the younger minds.

It appears that most of the present-time saints and priests have not cared to read and understand even basic school-level science, and so they usually fail to give a scientific response to the comments and logic of modernists and rationalists. Likewise, it appears that most of the modernists and rationalists have not cared to read and understand the philosophical base underlying the religion and its associated practices from some reliable source. They possibly obtained some superficial knowledge about these from some fraudulent religious practitioners who cheat gullible people. As a result, these modernists and rationalists have a poor understanding of the religion and its associated practices, which makes them declare these as unscientific and orthodox. The notions of both these groups are doing tremendous harm to the people in general. On one hand, the credibility of the ancient sages and the religion is at a loss for being dubbed as unscientific and orthodox. This, in turn, leads to a loss of national pride in the country and its heritage among the brilliant young minds, who get oriented towards the western lifestyle and western universities for studies and even jobs. This is leading to a regular brain drain in the country. On the other hand, the fraudulent religious practitioners get support from the misleading nonscientific counter-arguments of the other genuine saints and priests defending the religion, and thereby continue cheating the gullible people. Therefore, it is desirable to examine the issues that are leading to misconceptions about the religion.

1.5.1 Search for Scientific Proof

Rationalists and modernists search for some scientific proof of the existence of the supernatural power or ISHWARA. Their contention is that the creation and governance of nature and the universe is done by some scientifically-operating natural laws. Therefore, supernatural power has no role to play in the creation and governance of nature and the universe. Science so far has discovered some material energies as the fundamental forces operating inside an inert atom and the living cell. These energies can be captured through some scientific instrument in the form of some material element such as a particle or wave or an electric charge. Therefore, rationalists and modernists clamor for some similar type of material proof for the existence of the supernatural power or ISHWARA, which could be captured through some scientific instrument and mathematically explained. In fact, we are all so heavily engrossed in the material world these days that truth and rationality are understandable to most of us only through physical perception via the five sensory organs. So, the metaphysical realization through mental perception and intuitive vision does not appeal to be the reality to them.

But this abstract nonmaterial conceptualization through mental perception does sometimes become the reality. There are emotions, opinions, intuition, willpower, urges and similar concepts that we sometimes experience and realize in our fully awakened cognizance in life. However, these do not have any material proof that can subsist for being measurable by some energy device. The physiological functioning of the brain, being a material part, is governed by some biochemical functions, explaining the roles of neurons, electric impulses, hormones, etc., and their functioning can be mapped as material proof through various new medical devices. But, besides the physical functioning of the brain, the functioning of the mind is also governed by conscience and consciousness, both of which are nonmaterial and abstract realities. Therefore, scientific realities and abstract realizations both influence mental perceptions. This is why two persons get different perceptions of the same event despite both of them having similar backgrounds in education, social and material status. In fact, the material world is bound by the abstract nonmaterial limit not only in human behavior but also in the universe and in space as brought out by the most recent research in physics, which states that the universe is not real. It is the observer whose perception describes the reality. This was already propounded as a metaphysical concept in the religion by the ancient rishis. Since the physical sciences deal with only physical matter, the search for material proof may be sufficient sometimes for the scientific validity of physical matters. However, the material search for scientific validity in metaphysical concepts is surely a misconception.

Even the material proof of some physical science discoveries established earlier at some point in time has changed over time. For example, the earlier discovery of sub-atomic particles of electrons, protons and neutrons having a certain mass later ended in an immeasurable quantum field of energy. Likewise, the earlier concept of gravity as an invisible force that pulls objects with mass towards each other was later modified as the force generated by space curvature due to warps as bends and curves in the space fabric of the universe. Both these examples indicate that the material proof earlier sought for these discoveries needed further investigation, leading to their better theorizations; but again, without any measurable material proof of the quantum field of energy and space curvature. In the same way, the formation of a wide and diverse universe as a random occurrence after cooling down of an enormous amount of widely scattered radiation thrown out by the BIG BANG is a big postulation without any material proof. The theory of the BIG BANG explains only about five percent of the universe, leaving a big void about the remaining 95 percent as dark matter and dark energy. Further, scientists and rationalists explain that everything in nature is governed by the natural laws, which have come into operation by various forces like gravity, electro-magnetic and nuclear forces. But how these forces came into being after the BIG BANG is still a curiosity for both scientists as well as general people. Therefore, the argument of the non-availability of any scientific proof, de facto material proof, for the existence of any supernatural power or ISHWARA is simply a misconception about the religion.

1.5.2 Search for Scientific Development

Another misconception about the religion relates to a false presumption that all scientific knowledge useful for modern living, growth and development has been developed by modern science, while the religion and ancient knowledge have led to primitive developments and orthodox living. In fact, the findings of modern science, mostly made by western scientists in Europe and the USA, are relatively more recent and written mostly in the English language, which is spoken in a large part of the world. Most of the modern technologies influencing modern living are based on the findings of modern science. Hence, modern science is better known, read and talked about these days. But ancient Vedic knowledge and religion were developed by the ancient rishis of India more than several millenniums ago in the then-spoken Sanskrit language, which was unknown in other parts of the world. In those times, there were only a few civilizations developed in the world and these were widely scattered and had their own languages. Over time, the Sanskrit language was almost lost to antiquity due to several foreign invasions in the country and the enforcement of other foreign languages like Persian, Arabic, Urdu, English, etc., especially during the last millennium. Hence, the ancient Vedic knowledge of India remained unknown to the world. Despite foreign dominance, ancient Vedic knowledge, though not in the public domain, was somehow preserved by practicing the tenets and rites of the religion and other socio-religious customs in homes and temples with the help of some priests who knew the Sanskrit language. After the independence of the country, the Sanskrit language was revived and the ancient religious scriptures of Vedas and others were translated and published in Hindi, English and other regional languages.

In the late 20th century and early 21st century, there have been several attempts to rediscover the pronouncements of the ancient theologians from the Vedas and other scriptures so as to bring ancient thoughts and discoveries to the people. There are several books written by eminent writers that cover either some particular aspect or the complete academic achievements of the Vedic scholars. Among these, a recent book (Mathur, P.C., 2016) enumerates several thoughts of the ancient sages that are quite similar to some modern scientific discoveries. These ancient scientific thoughts were stated in verses (hymns) in the Sanskrit language in a spiritualistic manner in the form of prayers, practices and rituals to be followed as Dharma (duty) in the religion. The ancient scientific propositions were coded in these verses for prayers and rituals in words, which after proper decoding reproduced some mathematical number or some scientific thought. This coded presentation helped protect the misuse of implicit scientific knowledge by undesirable persons for selfish interests.

Quoting from the Atharva Veda (5.15), the book (Mathur, P.C., 2016) elucidates that the concept of Zero (Shoonya) and its application in developing higher series of numbers up to trillions, Vedic Mathematics (Shulbh Sutras) as treatises on mathematics to do complex calculations without computers and the concept of Infinity (Anant) to which no mathematical operation could be applied were all developed in ancient India. Quoting from Yajur Veda (17.2), the book states that the ancient sages used the word fire for radiation, ishtika for quanta and shenvaha for the energy of radiation in explaining that it is the quanta of radiation energy that pervades the entire observable universe, a concept similar to the recently discovered quantum theory in science. The book further enumerates that Beejganit as algebra, Jyamiti as geometry, and Trikonmiti as trigonometry were invented in India around 350 AD. Surya Siddhant is a treatise on trigonometry and Pingala (Chandahshastra 8.23) evolved binary numbers in the second century AD. Likewise, Baudhayana Shulbhsutra described the value of pi as 3 (ratio of the circumference to the diameter of a circle) around 500 BC, which was corrected up to four decimal places by the ancient sages in 500 AD. Likewise, the time taken by earth to complete a full revolution around the sun had been calculated as 365.258756848 days in the ancient period, while about 1,500 years later, the modern scientific measurement came to be 365.2596, with a negligible difference of about 0.00085 days.

Similarly, the book (Mathur, P.C., 2016) also mentions that the world's first surgeon, Sushrat, was born in India in 600 BC with a specialization in plastic surgery. Also, ancient sages discovered that everything in the universe emits radiation. Based on this knowledge, they developed Jyotirvigyan, which covers astronomy and cosmology, dealing with the radiations emitted by planetary and star constellations. They knew that everything in the universe was in constant motion, the study of which enabled them to make predictions of important natural events for public cause, e.g., weather forecasting for agriculture. Also, sonic science was highly developed in ancient India, based on which sages wrote mantras whose every word produced a particular vibration. The words of a mantra collectively form an octave that synchronizes with the biorhythm of the body and enhances its quantum. This enhanced biorhythm makes different psychic impacts on different individuals, giving them pleasure and confidence or solace and relief as desired. Thus, the book highlights several scientific thoughts of ancient India, which very well compare with those of modern science.

Besides full books, some individuals and socio-religious organizations have also written short articles that attempt to describe the glorified history of academic developments in the ancient period of the country, and these are available on the internet. Srinivasan Chakrapani (2022), after recently visiting the Samskrita Bharati institution in Bengaluru, found that ancient Vedas were orally conserved there and students of the Vedic school could continuously recite Vedic material for 240 hours. Also, Vedic literature was written on palm leaves, which was rewritten before the leaves decayed. He then wrote a readers' web blog in Times Now, briefly describing some scientific developments contributed by the ancient sages. In his short article, he presents many examples of ancient Vedic knowledge from the fields of astronomy, agriculture, physical and biological sciences, medical science and engineering, which are quite similar to the discoveries of modern science. In his article, he also recorded how some of the modern scientists like Heisenberg, Schrodinger and others have appreciated and favorably commented on Vedic knowledge. A religious organization, Hindu Janajagruti Samiti (2002), has prepared quite an elaborate literature in both Hindi and English languages on the scientific developments made by the ancient sages of the country. One such article describes the individual contributions of about ten famous ancient sages. The information obtained from the 'YouTube' video of this article of the Hindu Janajagruti Samiti is presented in the summary form in English in the appendix table. The facts presented in the appendix table indicate that the ancient think tank of sages/rishis had developed knowledge in almost all the disciplines that modern scientists have recently been exploring. Quite a similar commentary has also been made by Srinivasan Chakrapani (2022) in his readers' blog.

As for the impact of scientific development on the living patterns of people in the ancient period, the rishis advocated and guided a natural non-resisting path for growth and development to make it more sustainable in the long run and avoid the wrath of nature in the future, as already explained in section 1.4. Then, in order to operationalize this strategy, they also advocated simple living for the people in general and accorded a status of deities to all the elements of nature as DHARMA (duty) of the religion. Both these strategies are covered in more detail in sections 2.2.2, 3.2.1, 4.1 and 4.2. These strategies worked very well for several millenniums. The people lived a simple life in harmony with nature. There was no pollution, no adulterated food and no problem of social security. There was no tension for education, jobs, retirement, housing, entertainment, etc. They ate pure food and drank pure water, breathed pure air and led a stress-free life, which protected them from the modern lifestyle diseases. There were show-offs and showbiz but without the gimmicks and glamour of technology. This was the concept of happy well-being in austere living without the gadgets of the latest technology. All this continued until recent times when the western model of active and aggressive growth and development was adopted and practiced, which is now leading to the degradation of our natural resources due to over-exploitation. This western growth and development model is also leading to severe pollution, causing health hazards and diseases like cancer and heart attack, the wrath of nature in terms of uncontrollable climate change and an overall degradation of the environment not only in the country but all over the world.

1.5.3 Search for Scientific Validity

Rationalists and modernists generally search for scientific validity in everything. Therefore, they question the religious rites and customs by asserting that these cannot be explained by modern science and, hence, do not have scientific validity. Modern science has developed a great deal of knowledge on the various elements of and happenings in nature, which is called scientific knowledge. This scientific knowledge is logical, rational and verifiable through further experimentations/field observations. Hence, the program or practice proved right by known scientific knowledge is called logical and scientific. The program or practice proved wrong by known scientific knowledge is called illogical and unscientific. However, known scientific knowledge, though very large, is only a so-far discovered part of the infinite knowledge. Some programs or practices may not withstand the test of scientific scrutiny in terms of either approval or disproval by any known scientific knowledge. Therefore, simply using the criteria of nonfulfillment of known scientific knowledge or lack of any scientific proof in judging and declaring any program or practice as illogical and unscientific is in itself not a justified logical and scientific approach. If any case is proved wrong by known scientific knowledge, then and only then can it be declared as illogical and unscientific. The other case that lacks scientific proof or is not explained by any known scientific knowledge needs further detailed investigation concerning some possibility of hitherto unknown scientific discovery or some other non-scientific wisdom underlying and justifying it. Science is a very important aspect of modern human living, but it is not all in life. The traditions, encompassing values like etiquette, gratitude, compassion, happiness, satisfaction, peace, solace, etc., are also important in framing the way of life, which may constitute the underlying non-scientific wisdom in such cases.

Based on the knowledge gathered, especially about the happenings in nature and society, people since ancient times have been developing their programs and practices to support their livelihood and intellectual pursuits. Over time, repeating these programs and practices became traditions, which were then passed on over generations. Such traditions that withstood the test of time without creating any social problem and/or adverse effect on the natural environment were regarded as full of wisdom. Some of these traditions also found an important place in the religious tenets, rites and customs. Since modern science was not discovered in ancient times, it is quite possible that some of these traditions and religious practices may not withstand strict scientific scrutiny. But these traditions and religious practices have served to fulfill the criteria of wisdom by protecting the social fabric or natural resource base and, hence, formed a part of the way of life.

In the same manner, some event or happening in nature or society may remain unexplained by any known scientific knowledge, but some people may have accepted such an event or happening as a divine element. To illustrate, some specific temple at some specific place, some specific component of nature like a particular hill or river or some specific person like a sage may sometimes be regarded by the people as a divine element bestowed with a special divine energy of the supernatural power/ISHWARA, and may be revered and worshiped by them. Known scientific knowledge, which can test only the material energy, may not be able to prove—either right or wrong—the existence of any special divine energy in such a specific place or item or person. Therefore, the worship practice of such places, items, events or persons, though not supported by but also if not disproved by any known scientific knowledge, need be treated simply as a tradition based on the divine element and not just an illogical orthodox. The concept of divinity is often a corollary to the religion. Over time, such divinity becomes a tradition that is followed by the people. The following well-known example may help illustrate this divinity concept becoming a tradition, as also the orthodoxy therein, if and when noticed.

For example, the water of the river GANGES is believed to have a divine element as it can be stored and preserved for several years without getting contaminated and spoiled, unlike any other water. So, people have accepted it as divine holy water and worship the river GANGA as a mother and use this water in holy preparations. Thus, it has become a tradition. However, no well-tested scientific explanation has been attempted for this exclusive property of the GANGA water being germicidal, and this property has remained so over the millenniums. In fact, water gushing from two hot water springs, possibly sulfur springs, one at KEDARNATH and the other at BADRINATH, both in the state of UTTARAKHAND, also flows into the river GANGA. But this fact alone does not fully add to the germicidal property of the river water because several other large tributaries with tremendous amounts of gushing water also get mixed with the river. So, the sulfur content in this water, if any, gets highly diluted almost to the level of becoming lower than the Nano level, even lesser than that in high power Homoeopathic medicines, which are not considered as a cure but only as a placebo effect by allopathic doctors and many scientists. Several other rivers flowing from the same glaciers and hills such as the river JAMUNA do not possess this germicidal property. Therefore, the tradition of worshipping the river GANGA serves as a case of divine worship.

However, over the past several decades, a lot of industrial sludge and other pollutants along with household discharges have been and are still being dumped into the river GANGA. As a result, the GANGA water is now highly polluted and not fit for even bathing, particularly down the hills. This too is well known to people through the periodic media reports of the several GANGA cleaning programs initiated by the government and other international agencies. But a lot of people, including saints and priests, still believe in the divinity of the GANGA and the holiness of its water and continue its use for holy rituals. So, this has surely now become an orthodox ritual and needs to be discouraged, or else the divinity of the river water be restored urgently through expeditious GANGA water cleaning and by restricting any further inflow of industrial sludge and other pollutants in it. Further, besides industrial and household effluents, the river GANGA is also being polluted with a lot of puja/worship materials like flowers, leaves, paper, plastics and idols of deities immersed in it as these materials are considered sacred by the people. This is also not a rational practice but an orthodox ritual.

Likewise, there may be several other examples that people may regard as a divine power. Cases of extrasensory perceptions (ESP) are often reported in the press. Some individuals are found to exhibit extrasensory perception. They visualize unforeseen events and even make predictions. This has been called parapsychology, but no scientific knowledge has so far been discovered either to support or disprove this extrasensory perception. Some scientists, both in

India and abroad, have attempted investigations in cases of parapsychology, telepathy, thought-reading, etc., but could not discover any known scientific reason to support or disprove them. So, people considered it (ESP) as a divine power possessed by some exceptional person. Many Indian sages, western soothsayers and even some common individuals have been reported to have exhibited extrasensory perception. Likewise, cases of telepathy and premonition, owing to their occasional occurrences in reality, also fall into this category of divine power in the absence of any scientific explanation. Such traditions need to be carefully investigated and judged instead of being outright declared orthodox. In fact, traditions are schools that impart the knowledge that formal schooling does not include in its syllabus or books. Many modern and scientific persons often use some divine concepts like "O my GOD; GOD bless you; or touch wood," etc. Therefore, if some religious practice or tradition can be proved wrong by known scientific knowledge, only then it can be termed orthodox. In fact, fraudsters befooling the gullible need to be checked. People need to be informed about the possible loopholes in any tradition for befooling them and must be taught ways to protect themselves from fraud, instead of outrightly declaring the tradition itself as unscientific and orthodox.

CHAPTER

02 VEDIC SANATAN RELIGION

2.1 GENESIS

The ancient theological thinkers in India were sages called rishis. These rishis were of two types – Maharshi and Rajarshi. The Maharshi used to live an ascetic life in forests, on hills and banks of rivers. He would do yoga and meditation, and ponder over nature and its various phenomena to discover knowledge of nature's beneficial aspects for humanity. The Rajarshi used to live in the kingdom as a counselor to the king. He would often visit and consult the Maharshi, carrying his knowledge for developing programs that would benefit the king and the people of the kingdom. These rishis observed some beneficial energy resources in nature, such as sun, fire, air and water. After deep contemplation, concentration and meditation on harmonized and sustainable use and preservation of these energy resources, they conceptualized these as deities/devas. They conceived some mantras (hymns) and practices containing certain rituals for the reverence and worship of these deities/devas, to express gratitude to them for the harmonized use of these energies by the people. They included these mantras, practices and rituals in the first religious scripture known as the RIGVEDA. Later, four Vedas—named as RIGVEDA, SAMAVEDA, YAJURVEDA and ATHARVAVEDA—were composed in the then-spoken Sanskrit language. Vedas mean knowledge and are the earliest religious scriptures that contain ancient knowledge on nature, theology and way of life for human beings.

According to old historians, these Vedas were composed around 2000 BCE. Some recent historians estimate this Vedic period to be around 5000 BCE, or even earlier, based on carbon dating and the genealogical study of findings of some more recent excavations in several other parts of the country. The concept and matter of these Vedas were heard by several rishis during their deep meditations as intuitive voices called divine voices and, hence, were termed as SHRUTI (heard) knowledge. This SHRUTI knowledge was later remembered by others as SMRUTI (remembered) knowledge. It was much later that these Vedas were formally written in the Sanskrit language on paper, which was then developed from the bark of some special trees. In deep meditation, one gets completely detached from the ambiance and the self, and becomes thoughtless and transcendental. Then the inner consciousness gets linked with the Supreme consciousness i.e., supernatural power, and the intuitive voice heard is the divine voice of ISHWARA. In fact, this was also the case in some other major ancient religions as well. The MESSIAH JESUS heard the divine voice of GOD and scripted the new testaments, which became part of the holy BIBLE. The PAIGAMBER MOHAMMAD heard the divine voice of ALLAH and scripted the holy KURAN. However, in the case of the Vedas, it was not a single rishi who heard the divine voice, but several rishis who heard several divine voices. Then, these were discussed amongst the other rishis in SHASTRARTHA (academic discussion) to reach a consensus, before being incorporated into various Vedic scriptures.

Initially, the rishis' thinking and meditation were more focused on the worship of some deities/devas as being the important resources of energy, such as sun, fire, air and water, and it formed the subject matter of the initial scripture – the RIGVEDA. Gradually, their thinking and meditation covered several other aspects dealing with the physical, philosophical and theological descriptions of the universe, nature and human existence. More specifically, these other aspects dealt with the elements of nature and their various phenomena, creation and control of nature and the universe, concept of religion, purpose of life, ceremonies required for religious and virtuous living, dharma or duties for a way of life and social order, etc. Ancient thoughts and knowledge on all such aspects formed the subject matter of the ancient scriptures of the four Vedas and 108 Upanishads. Each Veda consists of four parts. The first part is Samhita, containing Mantras in the form of hymns, i.e., mantras of praise in reverence to ISHWARA and other deities/devas. The second part is Brahmana, containing text starting with reverence to ISHWARA and other deities but mainly dealing with KARMA KANDS, i.e., religious rites and customs, and directions about the use and conduct of various ceremonies. The third part is Aranyaka, containing text on JYAN (wisdom) and philosophy. The fourth part is the Upanishad, containing various discourses from several rishis on meditation, philosophy and spiritual knowledge. In ancient times, there used to be a fourth part—Up-Veda or Tantrum—dealing with science and practical instructions based on occult knowledge. But the rishis did not find it suitable for the common people and did not propagate it, and has, therefore, largely disappeared.

The Upanishads, also known as Vedanta, are the end part of the different Vedas. Each Veda has several Upanishads conceived and delivered (as discourses) by different rishis on different matters emerging from the contents of the respective Vedas. So, there are about 108 Upanishads, out of which only 11 are most common in use and reference. These Upanishads contain more elaborate meanings and guidance in the use and application of philosophical and theological knowledge of the concerned Veda, e.g., elaboration on the nature of the supreme BRAHMAN, the separated self, the universe, rebirth and liberation, religious doctrine and tenets. They also contain useful mantras and practices for the reverence and worship of ISHWARA and various other deities, a ceremony of HAVAN (burning some sacred incense on fire), self-enlightenment, various practices prescribed as DHARMA (duty) to be followed as a way of life for virtuous, compassionate and cohesive living, for maintaining social order, etc. In fact, the Upanishads serve better to provide understandable knowledge because the text in the other parts of the Vedas is very difficult to understand for general readers; only accomplished rishis or priests can understand the original text. These Vedas served to provide the philosophical base for the genesis of the Vedic Sanatan religion.

2.2 BASIC RELIGIOUS IDEAS

There is a good deal of literature available both online and offline on the Vedas and Hindu religion. Original versions of the ancient scriptures are in the Sanskrit language. Although some translations and commentaries on these are available in Hindi, English and other regional languages, they generally suffer from secondhand interpretations, making a good selection out of these a difficult choice. Thus, the incompetence of the present author in the Sanskrit language served as a big hurdle in obtaining original reliable knowledge of the Vedic Sanatan religion. Fortunately, the Board of Trustees of the Central Hindu College, Benares, India (1916)—now Benares Hindu University—had published a book on SANATAN DHARMA in the English language, an elementary textbook of HINDU RELIGION AND ETHICS, which is a complete treatise on the Vedic Sanatan religion, including respective Sanskrit Slokas from various ancient scriptures. The book, compiled by various scholars, contains Basic Hindu Religious Ideas in part-I, General Hindu

Religious Customs and Rites in part-II and Ethical Teachings in part-III. The book was digitized (a total of 322 pages) for the MICROSOFT Corporation by the Internet Archive in 2007 from the University of California Libraries. The book is now available both online and offline. This book has been used as the basic reference material in the present chapter. The Basic Hindu Religious Ideas (part-I) and General Hindu Religious Customs and Rites (part-II) of the above book, which deal with the main religious doctrine, tenets and rites, are summarized (shown in italics) in various sub-sections of the present chapter. These two parts of the book form the core of the Vedic Sanatan Religion. Vedic means derived from the Vedas and Sanatan means eternal, i.e., timeless for being followed since ancient times. Later, the Vedic Sanatan Religion came to be known as Hindu Religion the world over. The term Hindu was earlier used by the Arabs and Persians for the residents of the ancient SINDHU valley civilization of the country and was later adopted by others as well.

The summaries from the English text in each of the two parts (part-I and part-II) of the above-mentioned book on SANATAN DHARMA are presented here in section 2.2 and its sub-sections (2.2.1 to 2.2.6) and section 2.3 and its sub-sections (2.3.1 to 2.3.7) in italics in the first paragraph. Thereafter, the science and wisdom in each sub-section are examined, which appear in the following paragraph(s) written in a normal font. The part-III of the book mainly deals with ethical teaching, and therefore, has not been covered in the present book for brevity. Summarization of the original very long text in only one paragraph in each subsection (as shown in italics) has been done for brevity in the presentation of only the basic religious idea. This summarization helped save and devote more space for the presentation of the science and wisdom search therein, which is the main objective and purpose of the present book. In this summarization, if there remains any flaw, it may be deemed as an incomprehensibility of the author of the present book and, if pointed out, will be thankfully accepted for correction in future reprints.

Modern science is only the recent development of knowledge and as such it did not exist in ancient times. But the religious doctrine, tenets and customs do contain some logical thoughtfulness based on ancient logic and wisdom. Therefore, at some places in the text, some modern science discoveries have been mentioned and related to some ancient thought only to show that the ancient thought did contain a similar meaning and connotation as that of the modern science discovery. The objective is not to compare them, but only to co-relate a similarity in thoughtfulness and purpose, and to bring out the scientific connotation in ancient thought. Wherever possible, this linking of some specific ancient thought with some specific modern science thought is done only to show that the ancient thought is not unscientific and orthodox, and that some sort of scientific thinking is inherently visible in the specific ancient thought too.

2.2.1 The One Existence

The religion believes that 'There is one Infinite, Eternal, Changeless Existence, One and the ALL. From THAT all comes forth, to THAT all returns. There is "One only, without a second." That includes within Itself all that ever has been, is and can be.' The universe is a manifestation of the Existence. "ALL this verily is BRAHMAN." He is also called NIRGUN BRAHMAN, i.e., being formless without attribute. He is also called ISHWARA, or PUROSHOTTAMA, or the Supreme Spirit, The Self. As Spirit, He reveals the other side of ALL, which is named as Prakriti or matter which takes all sorts of forms, shapes and kinds. The matter is JADAM or inert without consciousness and can be perceived by the senses as it can take some form. But Spirit cannot be perceived as it is formless. It is Spirit that is life that thinks, feels and observes, and is one and the same in everybody and everything. Spirit has three qualities, Sat, Chit and Anand, i.e., truth, consciousness and bliss. Matter also has three qualities, Tamah, Rajah and Sattvam, i.e., inertia, mobility and rhythm. The Divine power of ISHWARA is the SHAKTI, which makes matter begin to take form, is called MAYA. In short, He is the source for all creation and to which all creation returns. It is not just matter. It is also spirit, the living force, and called ATMA, the most powerful. An extremely small subtle part of this ATMA, i.e., an ANSHAH, is called JIVA, which is found in all its creation, living or non-living.

The above conceptualization of BRAHMAN or ISHWARA is the main doctrine of the religion. The conception of one infinite, eternal, changeless, formless and all-pervading attribute indicates BRAHMAN to be the super energy that is the source of all creation and to which all returns. In fact, nothing else, other than the super energy concept, could match this conception of BRAHMAN. Only, it was described in different words of the Sanskrit language. Therefore, BRAHMAN has to be conceptualized as an infinite, formless eternal source of energy. Thus, this religious concept is fully in consonance with the latest scientific discovery on the ultimate constituent of the universe. So, there is nothing unscientific and orthodoxy in it. The religion's finding that "there is one infinite, eternal, changeless and formless existence, which is the source of all creation and to which all creation returns" is quite similar to the search of modern science for the ultimate constituent of which the whole universe is made up. The findings of the religion and the search of modern science both have converged on what constitutes all creation in the universe, i.e., infinite formless energy. Only the process of reaching and the language of stating these inferences are different in religion and science.

Modern science has been searching for the ultimate building blocks of matter and the universe for a long time. Earlier, science believed an atom to be the smallest form of matter. Later, sub-atomic particles of electrons, protons and neutrons were discovered as the constituents of an atom. Much later, through Large Hadron Collider (LHC) experiments, a whole set of many sub-atomic massless particles were found to be revolving inside an atom. Then, the physicists discovered various energy fields operating inside an atom and also in space. All these energy fields were found to be mutually interactive and deeply entangled with each other. This led to the conceptualization of a quantum fields of energy existing all around in space since the Big Bang. They found these quantum fields to be formless, infinite with real fluid-like substance with quanta of energy, showing ripples and waves bubbling and fluctuating in multiple dimensions (David Tong, 2017). These quantum fields gives mass to other massless particles of the atom, thereby becoming the source for all creation.

Thus, the latest findings of modern science about an all-pervading, infinite, formless quantum fields of energy as the constituent of the universe is quite similar to the Vedic Sanatan religion's concept of BRAHMAN as one infinite, eternal, changeless and formless existence, which is the source of all creation and to which all creation returns. However, there is one big difference between the findings of science and that of the religion. Science does not believe in spirit and considers only matter as the constituent of the universe. But the concept of BRAHMAN in the religion is not just matter but is also spirit—the living force. The religion believes that matter is inert without consciousness, is perceived by senses, and is called Prakriti, having qualities of inertia, mobility and rhythm. In religion, spirit is the life that can think, feel and observe, and is the same in everybody and everything. It is the SHAKTI, the divine power, which makes matter take form, shape and kind, and is called MAYA. Spirit has the qualities of truth, consciousness and bliss, i.e., it is the truth that exists (all others change in form, shape and kind); it is consciousness that can think, feel and observe; and it leads to realization of bliss, which is perpetual inner happiness.

While investigating the quantum field, some physicists described quantum fields to be nonmaterial in nature (Mani Bhaumic, 2021). Other physicists did not take note of it perhaps because their minds were deeply rooted in the investigation of the matter particles. But the observations of 'real fluid-like substance with quanta of energy, showing ripples and waves bubbling and fluctuating in multiple dimensions' indicate pulsation that is a characteristic feature of the living force, which substantiates the observation of the 'nonmaterial element' as mentioned above. Hence, this observation in the LHC experiments also indicates the presence of living energy in the universe. The ancient rishis had already conceptualized BRAHMAN not just as matter but also as spirit—the most powerful living force. This living force is present everywhere in a subtle form as ANSHAH of BRAHMAN, and they called it JIVA. This JIVA, being the subtle form of BRAHMAN, is not simply material energy but also the living force. This JIVA creates life by activating the replicating material energy—say DNA of modern science—whenever and wherever formed or already present, as explained in section 1.3 in more detail. The religion conveys this in very simple terms to the common people that life is created by the ISHWARA.

2.2.2 The Many

All creation of NIRGUN BRAHMAN, i.e. JIVA, passes through three distinct stages of creation, preservation or growth, and dissolution or destruction, which are all material attributes. Therefore, NIRGUN BRAHMAN got revealed into three SAGUN or SAKAR manifestations called TRIMURTY of BRAHMA, VISHNU and SHIVA to cause a BRAMHANDOM: the attribute of BRAHMA as creator, VISHNU as preserver and SHIVA as destroyer. BRAHMA, the creator, first shaped the matter into seven Tattva or elements, viz., pure reason, egoism, ether (sky), air, water, fire and earth, out of which all things were made. Next, ten Indriyas (centers of senses) in form of the five senses of smell, taste, sight, touch and hearing, and five their respective organs of nose, tongue, eyes, skin and ears were created. Then, five centers of action, viz., hands, feet, speech, generation and excretion, and then finally the mind to think over all the sensations and actions was created. Next, Brahma created Devas, also called Suras, to administer and manage the laws of ISHWARA. Next, He also created Asuras as enemies of Devas. These creations were all wrapped with the Gunas of Sattvaguna, Rajoguna and

Tamoguna, operating in varying degrees and effects in different forms of creations. Then Brahma created minerals, plants, animals and men. This completed the picture of a universe, wherein unfolding of the powers of the JIVA, i.e., evolution, was to take place through activation of the physical forms created by Brahma. This activation was the work of Vishnu who breathed life, as Prana, into all these forms and the consciousness. For the life creation, Vishnu made several divine manifestations as Avatars starting from Matsya (fish) to Kurma (tortoise), Varaha (boar), Narasimha (man-lion), Vamana (dwarf man), Parashurama (Rama of axe), Ramachandra (virtuous model king), Krishna (manifestation of divine love and wisdom), Buddha (teacher of truth – Nirvana through austerity), and Kalki in the future (to close this cycle of evolution). The third aspect of dissolve of the JIVAS was the work of Shiva, calling them to union with BRAHMAN.

This tenet has the scientific connotation that everything passes through three distinct stages of creation, preservation and destruction. This is a scientific fact not only for all living beings but also for all inert matter including planets, stars, galaxies and even the universe. The religion believes that these three stages of creation, preservation and destruction, being the material attributes, are governed by the three SAKAR revelations of the NIRGUN BRAHMAN called the trinity of BRAHMA, VISHNU and SHIVA respectively as creator, preserver and destroyer. This SAKAR revelation would facilitate better understanding by the common people about how the NIRGUN BRAHMAN regulates the material world through its personified powers in the form of this trinity called the three BHAGWANS for regulating the material functions of creation, preservation and destruction. This helped make the religion acceptable to the common people for their mundane matters, as explained later in the next paragraph. The rest of the tenet is a postulation about how BRAHMA created everything in the universe and VISHNU created life, which is a mythological narration of evolution on earth for the understanding of the common people.

But the concept of BRAHMAN revealed as the trinity for the common people does have a remarkable philosophical underlining with several elements of wisdom. The ancient theologians aimed at making the religion acceptable to the common people as a self-realization and not as an imposed religious doctrine. This helped in developing a sustainable social base for the religion. This made the concept of BRAHMAN better understood and more useful instead of simply remaining a theological ideology. In developing the religion's acceptability by the people, three objectives were implicitly incorporated through a threefold approach adopted. First – to make religion a workable solution for worship to seek benevolence and solace, second – to make religion a way of life for them, and third – to make people passive believers of the religion. The basic conception of formless NIRAKAR BRAHMAN or ISHWARA was found to be too difficult to grasp for worship by the common people who were grossly engrossed in mundane matters. The NIRAKAR BRAHMAN would better appeal to sages and rishis engaged in theological pursuits. The ancient thinkers realized that the common people would believe and worship ISHWARA for the fulfillment of their mundane materialistic desires. So, they would need a materialistic and visible ISHWARA with whom they could develop a sense of belonging and worship to seek benevolence. Therefore, SAKAR BRAHMAN was visualized as BRAHMAN revealed for the view of the common people and to serve as the workable solution for worship. This SAKAR revelation was in the form of the Trinity of BRAHMA, VISHNU and SHIVA, respectively for creation, preservation and dissolution functions in the evolution process of everything in the universe. This was done to fulfill the first objective of developing a workable solution for worship to seek benevolence and solace.

Making religion a way of life was the second objective to be achieved while making religion acceptable to the common people. This was a great energy-saving as well as environment-preserving philosophy of the religion. The ancient theologian rishis thought of making religion the way of life so that people, after their daily routines of washing, meals, avocation, rest and sleep, spent their leisure time in religious activities like doing daily worship rituals, celebrating religious festivals, singing BHAJANS/hymns, reading/listening or discussing religious stories and epics, etc. A great deal of rites and rituals for several socio-religious activities and festivities were developed and prescribed, which would involve a considerable part of their free time. Also, various Puranas and Epics containing stories of exciting achievements, virtuous living and melodrama were conceived and developed to absorb the minds of the people in their available leisure time through readings and discussions on these stories. All this was expected to make the religion a way of life as well.

This religious orientation of the life of common people is aimed at making every individual believe in and depend on ISHWARA for everything in life and accept all achievements as a merciful benevolence from ISHWARA. This would make them shun all sense of egoism and conflict. It was thought that this would help develop a better social ambiance with a compassionate, cohesive and civilized society. Further, simple living was considered more sustainable, low energy consuming and more environment protective. So, simple living was advocated and propagated for the common people as a religious way of living. Thus, religious orientation, together with simple living, made the religion a way of life. The concept of simple living did not mean ascetic living with a bare minimum, instead, it meant austere living by conserving scarce resources and avoiding all wasteful ostentations. It was thought that simple living would develop a more egalitarian society, which would help preserve the social ambiance in the long run. Simple living would also lead to very low energy requirements and, thereby, save the natural resources and protect the natural environment from any damage by developmental activities in the long run. Thus, the philosophy of making the religion a way of life, through religious orientation and simple living, displays the great environmental concern in the religion, which did help in maintaining the social ambiance as well as in protecting the natural environment for more than two millenniums. This continued until recently when religious fervor greatly declined due to modern living with ostentations, which has led to severe damage in both social and natural environments.

Next, the introduction of the element of SAGUN ISHWARA in the form of the trinity of BRAHMA, VISHNU and SHIVA led to the introduction of idolatry in the religion, as idolized physical objects and images of these forms of ISHWARA were used in worship. The idolatry later expanded to a great level when idolized physical objects and images of several other deities were also gradually introduced. This idolatry attracted the most attention for censure and criticism by several modern sages as well as scientists and rationalists. However, it did help in making people passive believers of the religion, which was the third objective in the threefold approach adopted to make the religion acceptable to the people, as stated above. It was thought that practicing religion as the way of life, together with idolatry, would make people do regular prayers and worship the various idolized SAGUN forms of ISHWARA and/or other deities for seeking fulfillment of their mundane desires or solace in grief. In this way, people would develop a strong belief that ISHWARA and/or deities are all powerful, i.e., ALMIGHTY, not only in providing all sorts of providences and fulfilling desires but also in protecting themselves. This belief would make people passive believers and, thereby fulfill the third objective implicit in the threefold approach adopted for making religion acceptable to the common people, as stated earlier.

By becoming passive believers, people in general, would not show any adverse response to any act of blasphemy committed by others. They would leave it to the ALMIGHTY to pardon or punish the guilty. They would consider ISHWARA and the deities to be much more wise and powerful in showing a response to the blasphemous as compared to the weak and mortal ordinary human beings. Indeed, this did happen and is still happening by and large among the believers despite a lapse of several millenniums. But this attitude of passive belief does not diminish the belief of the people in the power of the ALMIGHTY; they continue their faith, prayer and worship as before. This shows magnanimity and not cowardice or weakness in avoiding unnecessary conflicts on account of blasphemy. Thus, the concept of NIRGUN BRAHMAN revelation into the SAKAR Trinity converted the theological ideology of the Vedic Sanatan religion into a social philosophy, having several desirable elements of wisdom such as, a religious way of life preserves the social ambiance and the natural resource base, and passive belief avoids unnecessary religious conflicts.

In fact, the conceptualization of visible trinity manifestations of ISHWARA also represents an admixture of the development processes associated with the three broad lifestyles prevalent in ancient times. One, the ascetic lifestyle with a bare minimum for sustenance as practiced by the sages and rishis who lived in hermitages on hills or banks of rivers and were generally devoted to spirituality, theology and the study of nature. Second, the austere lifestyle with only the essentials for living without any ostentatious wastefulness as practiced by the common people who lived in villages and urban areas, and were generally engaged in creative and productive activities in different avocations. Third, the aristocratic lifestyle with luxuries and comforts as practiced by well-to-do people like kings, courtiers and other noble persons who generally lived in urban areas, and were devoted to administration, welfare and counseling. Initially, the development process entailed some manual labor and some intelligence, which was provided by the common people; then some wealth as capital along with management, which was provided by the well-to-do aristocratic people; and then some skill and techniques for energy transformation, which was provided by the rishis living as ascetic sages.

The BRAHMA manifestation of ISHWARA as creator represents the providence for the endeavors of the common people living austere lives, generally engaged in creative and productive activities in their lives. Their endeavors required some intelligence and wisdom whose providence goddess is SARASWATI, associated as a consort with BRAHMA. The VISHNU manifestation of ISHWARA as preserver represents the providence for the endeavors of well-to-do people living aristocratic lives, engaged in administration, welfare and counseling activities in their lives. They provided capital and management to all development activities. For this, they needed wealth, whose providence goddess is LAKSHMI, associated as a wife with VISHNU, the providence for management and preservation. The SHIVA manifestation of ISHWARA as destroyer represents the providence for the endeavors of sages and rishis living ascetic lives, engaged in spirituality, theology and study of nature's phenomena. They discovered the knowledge from nature in terms of the manner and time of occurrence of the associated energy flows for human welfare. Then, they meditated and developed science and art, i.e., skills and techniques of utilizing sound, air, water and heat (fire) energy available in nature for useful purposes, i.e., transforming energy from one form and converting it into another form. Since they lived ascetic lives in forests or hills, there was very little possibility for modern tests and experiments as done in modern scientific investigations. The rishis and sages discovered such skills and techniques through deep meditation whose providence is SHIVA, usually meditating in the high KAILASH hills. The providence for energy is goddess PARVATI associated as a wife with SHIVA.

The worshipers and followers of the VISHNU avatar were known as Vaishnava, and they built several grand temples as they had tremendous wealth and support, especially from kings and other well-to-do people. There is a large number of grandeur temples in the country that relate to the Vishnu avatar. The worshipers and followers of the SHIVA avatar were known as Shaiva, and they also built some temples, mostly in the hills, through sculptures and paintings on hill rocks and caves made generally by rishis. Almost all the hill locations in the country have some temples relating to the SHIVA avatar. The common people had neither wealth nor time for the construction of temples for their providence, the BRAHMA avatar, as they were mostly busy managing their daily needs, and worshiped the VISHNU avatar or SHIVA avatar along with the well-to-do people or ascetic saints and sages in their respective temples, for seeking divine blessings for wealth or spirituality. So, there is only one temple of the BRAHMA avatar in the country, located in Pushkar, Rajasthan.

The manifestation of the SHIVA avatar as destroyer has another aspect too. When the entire developmental creativity and productivity on earth becomes futile on its own account of unscrupulous and unsustainable technology and development level and needs rejuvenation, then SHIVA takes the scene in the RUDRA avatar (form). SHIVA expresses the RUDRA form of His anger with a TANDAV dance, which generates an intense amount of heat, raising temperatures in and around the KAILASH hills that cause glaciers to melt, which leads to the great deluge. The great deluge destroys the entire developmental creativity. Thereafter, a fresh beginning for new creation starts and a new ERA of creation begins. The history of the complete vanishing of several great early civilizations, like the Maya of Central America and Mesopotamia of Central Asia several millennium years back, is testimony to destruction on their own accord of unscrupulous and unsustainable development. Developmental creativity must keep in mind the extent of exploitation of the local geophysical factors as also its impact on the natural environment so as to remain sustainable in the very long run. Otherwise, when the exploitation of natural resources exceeds their carrying capacity, dissolution is imminent as a part of the cycle of creation, growth and destruction. Thus, the concept of the visible Trinity of BRAHMAN is found to be full of wisdom and quite rational as it fully matches with developmental realities of both the past (ancient) and the present, only described as the mythology of the religion.

In brief, the mythology in the ancient VISHNU Purana describes the current ERA of creation, comprising four time periods of Satyuga, Tretayuga, Dwaparyuga and Kaliyuga. Then, it explains the ten incarnations of the VISHNU avatar, which demonstrate the stages of evolution of life on earth: first as fish for oceanic life, second as turtle for amphibian life, third as boar for landward life, fourth as NARSINGH – a beastly powerful human as half lion and half human, fifth as BALI showing dwarf – a proud and powerful human king, sixth as PARASHURAM showing a developed and powerful but angry and egoist human, all in the Satyuga period. The seventh incarnation as RAMA – a virtuous human with moral values in the Tretayuga period, eighth as KRISHNA showing a fully developed human with all requisite qualities of love and romance, diplomacy, warrior and guide in the Dwaparyuga period, ninth as GAUTAM BUDDHA showing complete renunciation for Nirvana, and the tenth of Kali for dissolution to be incarnated in the present segment of Kaliyuga. Thus, these mythological stories narrate in the simple way the story of evolution from oceanic creatures to land-based creatures to half-wild humans to gradually more and more reformed human beings for easy understanding of the common people. These stories are mythological narrations but quite logical in representing the evolution of life from water sources to landwards and finally to humans, and then a human's own gradual empowerment.

The mythology also describes that the VISHNU avatar, after creating the universe, found the planet earth quite suitable in terms of the required ambiance for further developmental activities of both animate and inanimate types. So, the VISHNU avatar created the BRAHMA avatar from his navel through vegetative reproduction (i.e., single body cell developed into full body) and asked him to initiate further developmental activities. As the BRAHMA avatar was created through vegetative reproduction, He created several vegetative reproductions of devas, rishis, devils (asuras), plants, animals, etc., who failed to accelerate further diverse types of developmental activities. He then created the SHIVA avatar to accelerate further developmental activities with diversities. The SHIVA avatar, after deep meditation, developed the concept of metamorphosis of energy from one form to another, which helped the creation of diversities. He also developed the concept of sexual reproduction through male and female cells by producing two sons, KARTIKEYA and GANESHA, with His wife PARVATI who is the Goddess of providence for energy, i.e., Shakti. This set the developmental ball self-rolling through sexual reproduction in all species. This shows why religious people worship the Shivalinga in India as a representation of sexual reproduction and the concept of a family. Through sexual reproduction and the concept of family, the associated emotions and urge for development began rolling. This transformation of energy and sexual reproduction led to the subsequent creation of a widely diversified and glamorous world of the day, which was described by the theologians as MAYA for not being real or sustainable but changing through metamorphosis.

These mythological stories only intend to show that the evolution process initially began with vegetative reproduction in terms of a living cell that developed into a living being, and later snowballed through sexual reproduction into male and female cells, before finally turning into a full-fledged evolution. There is nothing orthodoxy in it as it is the fact stated through fiction to make it more appealing as well as interesting to the common people. The story of evolution in a nutshell can be stated as: after the BIG BANG/or desire of ISHWARA VISHNU, a voluminous mass of exploding energy spread around everywhere in all directions. With the passage of time, it started cooling down, leading to the formation of galaxies, stars and planets, then the formation of various elements of matter, followed by air, water, heat and radiation, which generated a suitable climate for vegetative reproduction as captivated in the story of the BRAHMA avatar. Lastly, came sexual reproduction through male and female cells as captivated in the story of the SHIVA avatar. Except for the initial stage of BIG BANG/or desire of ISHWARA VISHNU, the rest of the stages are quite the same in both science and religion, except that in religion these are stated as mythological stories along with fiction. The stories have always served as a great medium to convey any message as well as pass the time. Even in the present scientific era, fictional stories of Batman, Spiderman, Harry Potter, etc. are best sellers all over the world, without any comment on their rationality by anyone. The stories, whether ancient or modern, serve the purpose of good pastime and entertainment. If these convey some message and inspiration, they become religious mythologies and part of the traditional repository of wisdom as well.

2.2.3 Re-birth

Every JIVA, i.e., an ANSHAH of NIRGUN BRAHMAN, passes through the three stages of creation or birth, then preservation or growth and finally of destruction or death. The JIVA in the non-living matter forms like rocks and stones is powerless and changes its form by the natural catastrophes like thunderstorms, floods, cyclones, etc., to become ores and minerals. It gradually improves its power further when it gets life to become plants (such as minerals in plants) and gets furthermore power when it becomes trees bearing fruits. Then gradually it passes through higher lives from micro-organisms to aquatics to birds, animal kingdom and finally to a human being in a series of rebirth cycles, such as minerals to plant/tree leaves and fruits, which are eaten by some living creatures to become flesh and milk, which are eaten by other living creatures and human beings and, thus, gradually improves its power in moving from one to another life form. When it acquires very high power in terms of becoming high quality of human life it finally goes to re-unite with the PARAMATMA and achieves MOKSHA, otherwise goes to more cycles of rebirth. Even after acquiring very high power, some JIVA may recontinue rebirth as Rishis or other virtuous humans as to help other JIVAs accelerate their empowerment.

This tenet of rebirth is a bit tricky to understand the implicit scientific undertone in it. As explained earlier in section 2.2.1, the superpower BRAHMAN is conceived as the grand big source of infinite formless energy, and JIVA as the subtle quanta of this energy spread in everything, everywhere all around the space. Both these theological concepts of BRAHMAN and JIVA of the religion are quite similar to the modern astrophysics concept of some Singularity leading to the BIG BANG and spread of the un-measurable volume of energy, which later formed the diverse universe. The BRAHMAN represents the Singularity of the infinite energy, which spreads itself in various subtle forms of JIVA, causing a very diverse universe through the cycles of rebirth of JIVA. Further, the ancient theologians also believed that the JIVA energy cannot vanish or be destroyed but can change its form through metamorphosis into something else; they called this change the rebirth of JIVA. This is how the great diversity exhibited in nature and the universe is produced, preserved and destroyed through JIVA taking rebirth in multiple forms through metamorphosis. Thus, the JIVA energy remains the same and it only changes into multiple forms through cycles of rebirth. This theological concept of JIVA of the religion is also quite similar to the modern sciences' first law of thermodynamics on the conservation of energy, which states that energy cannot be created or destroyed but can only change its form, thus, leading to new creation.

As stated above, the concept of the re-birth of JIVA implies its metamorphosis into another form of energy, and its empowerment in different forms depends upon the realized active potential of that form of energy. For example, as a subtle form of the BRAHMAN, JIVA may also exist in rock or stone form, but it has the lowest minimum power for lying in inertia in a remote place. But when it breaks down due to the impact of some natural catastrophe, like a thunderstorm or cyclone, it becomes a mineral that flows down with water. When it is absorbed by the plant or tree to become a fruit, as to make seeds for further reproduction of a plant or tree or to be eaten by some bird, animal or human, then it is re-birth of the JIVA from mineral to fruit, with some higher empowerment as the active potential of the mineral is realized. Likewise, when the fruit is eaten by some bird or animal or human, it changes into flesh, which is again the re-birth of JIVA with some more empowerment. In a similar manner, re-birth of the JIVA as an un-destructible subtle energy keeps on recurring through metamorphosis in different forms of stones or minerals or plants or trees or woods or micro-organisms or birds or animals or humans and anything new. The subtle energy, JIVA, remains the same undestroyed energy during its metamorphosis through various rebirth cycles. Thus, this tenet of the religion quite resembles the first law of thermodynamics, stating that energy cannot be created or destroyed, it only changes form. In case of the empowerment of JIVA in human beings, some mores and taboos were prescribed in the religion to make human living more righteous, virtuous and compassionate and, thereby further empower JIVA. A highly empowered JIVA in the human form was considered entitled to the ultimate moksha, in terms of re-union with the BRAHMAN, or the subtle energy uniting with the grand big source of infinite energy. Again, JIVA only changes form to unite with the original source of universal energy, i.e., BRAHMAN to achieve moksha, i.e., freedom from the cycle of rebirth.

The concept of moksha may seem to be quite a controversial myth to some modern and rational people who often look at anything only at the superficial level. But this moksha concept too has quite a similarity with the modern astrophysics concept of great energy condensed in a black hole, which further attracts and absorbs all the energy coming into it, and perhaps may become a Singularity in some very distant future. In a similar manner, the concept of moksha indicates that the subtle JIVA energy unites with the infinite energy of NIRGUN BRAHMAN, which is similar to the concept of singularity. This again brings out that science and wisdom are fully imbibed in the Vedic Sanatan religion, though stated in different words and languages. These similarities in ancient and modern thoughts are indicative of the fact that what ancient theologians devised as the Vedic Sanatan religion is not backward and illogical or orthodox but is quite logical, with pieces of wisdom and knowledge perfectly resembling that of the modern science theories, only both were expressed in different words and different languages. The ancient rishis conceptualized it through keen observations in nature and deep meditation thereafter. One is required to do deep meditation to discover such metaphysical knowledge implicit in the religion. Also, one should possess an unbiased mind and real knowledge of both, science and the religion. Superficial knowledge always generates a layman's comments.

2.2.4 Karma

Karma does not simply mean action. It includes three elements of desire, thought and action in that sequence. First there is desire which serves as the cause, then thought to fulfill desire and then action to fulfill the desire. There is cause and effect relation. Every action has its effect. Some actions bring good effect and are called good karma. Some actions bring bad effect and are called bad karma. To get moksha, JIVA must do good karma which means good thoughts and so, good desires. This serves as an inspiration for making only good desires, good thoughts and do good karma. This would make a good life and empower JIVA to finally unite with ATMA, and get rid of birth and death cycles. Bad karma would not empower JIVA which goes to rebirth again. Thus, desire, thought and karma altogether determine the cycles of birth and rebirth of JIVA.

This tenet is full of elemental wisdom as it simply advocates and inspires people for good karma through selfless desire, leading to pure and compassionate thoughts. Such advocacy forms part of the civil charter in the constitutions of all modern governments. Even if the concept of moksha, which in fact has a full scientific connotation as explained above in section 2.2.3, is detached from it, still this tenet is a desirable piece of wisdom that motivates good desires, good thoughts and good actions in people, leading to good karma for righteous, virtuous and compassionate living. Then, people's good karma would lead to a caring, compassionate and cohesive society, which would help preserve a better social ambiance in the long run. Thus, this tenet has a built-in concern for achieving the desired social ambiance by inspiring people to have good thoughts, good desires and good karma. This is true not only for individuals to get further empowerment for their onward journey after death but also for society to remain compassionate and cohesive for a better social milieu. Thus, this tenet represents good advocacy, full of elemental wisdom, which helps in preserving a good social environment besides empowering the soul for its next journey.

2.2.5 Sacrifice

The principle underlying all sacrifices is enunciated as follows. First, the creation itself is sacrifice. ISHWAR confines Himself in a subtle form in matter as JIVA in order that a universe may be made manifest. Thus, ISHWAR sacrificed Himself. This is the primary sacrifice on which the Law of sacrifice is based. This also enunciates the meaning of sacrifice as the pouring of one's life for the benefit of others. The JIVAS of the mineral kingdom break up their bodies for the support of JIVAS of plants and trees which, in turn, break up their bodies for the support of JIVAS of the animal kingdom and which, in turn, sacrifice their bodies for the support of JIVAS of other animals and human kingdom. Even JIVAS of the human kingdom rise to a higher self by sacrificing their bodies for the support of other human lives in war and catastrophe. This is called self-sacrifice and shows the divinity of the JIVA as an ANSHAH/subtle part of ISHWAR. In return for the sacrifice, JIVA receives the joy of being in a higher self and empowerment. Furthermore, these sacrifices bring forth that all lives are interdependent, and can only prosper sustainably through interdependence and coexistence. The Rishis taught humans to offer sacrifice to the Devas, to Rishis, to ancestors, and to other humans and animals as a repayment of the debt they owed to all these for their sacrifices, which led to the present being. This would evolve them to a higher self, and cultivate the faculties of gentleness, empathy and tenderness. Then, every action becomes a sacrifice to ISHWAR, paving the way for liberation or moksha.

This tenet is also full of elemental wisdom as it advocates the concept of sacrifice to be practiced by the people, which will empower not only the individual but also help in building a coherent, compassionate and evolutionary society. The present is an outcome of the past and will lead to the future. That's how the time element represents another dimension in evolution and creation besides the three physical dimensions of space, viz., length, breadth and height. There is no absolute independence in an evolutionary process. Howsoever grandeur the present be, it is built on the edifice of the past to which the present owes for its existence. Therefore, this tenet inspires people to make sacrifices as an expression of thankfulness as also a sort of payoff to the contribution and help rendered by several other people and other living beings in the past and present, which has made our lives simple and comfortable. This is the process of evolution in any progressive society. Such a realization is necessary where one's present achievements have been possible only due to the work and sacrifices made by many other living beings, both humans and non-humans. Therefore, one must make this due realization by doing some act of sacrifice for others. Such a realization and act of sacrifice will shun all feelings of superiority, egoism, undue pride and self-esteem from one's personality, thereby making one a caring human who avoids all social conflicts and follows peace and compassion. Thus, this tenet is also quite a desirable piece of wisdom as it aims at making people virtuous, polite and caring, and in turn, building a compassionate and coherent society to preserve the desired social environment in the long run.

2.2.6 The Worlds – Visible and Invisible

There are three LOKAS (worlds) in which JIVA (subtle energy) is bound to travel through the cycle of births and deaths. These LOKAS are: BHURLOKA – the visible physical world of earth, BHUVARLOKA – the invisible world as an intermediate between world and SVARG (heaven), and SVARGLOKA (the heaven). After birth, JIVA develops three sheaths (coverings) corresponding to these three LOKAS. These sheaths are: (i) ANNAMAYAKOSH – built up of eaten food and corresponds to the visible BHURLOKA, (ii) PRANAMAYAKOSH – contains PRANA, the life energy, and this also corresponds to BHURLOKA, (iii) MANOMAYAKOSH – this has two parts, the denser part of the sheath of passions corresponds to BHURLOKA, and the finer part, the sheath of emotions and thoughts, corresponds to SVARGLOKA. The physical body, also called as STHULA SHARIRA, is the same as ANNAMAYAKOSH. The subtle body, called as SHUKSHMA SHARIRA, includes both PRANAMAYAKOSH and MANOMAYAKOSH. After death, the SHUKSHMA SHARIRA is separated from STHULA SHARIRA, the latter left as lifeless matter. The JIVA remains in SHUKSHMA SHARIRA, and quickly shakes off PRANAMAYAKOSH. Then, the denser part of MANOMAYAKOSH remains as an outer garment of JIVA, which is now a PRETA inhabitant of PRETLOKA. If has been a good person on earth, JIVA passes away happily from this condition to its next journey, but if has been a bad person on earth, JIVA suffers as NARAK for a longer time in this condition of PRETLOKA. Then, the denser part of MANOMAYAKOSH falls away and JIVA goes as PITRI (ancestors) into PITRILOKA to purify the remaining MANOMAYAKOSH and finally goes to SVARGLOKA and enjoys the fruit JIVA has stored up through good conduct. After the SVARGLOKA time is over, JIVA if highly empowered, unites with the Supreme Self PARAMATMA, otherwise returns to BHURLOKA for rebirth. Even some highly empowered JIVAS return to BHURLOKA as rishis, saints and other virtuous men with wisdom to guide and help other JIVAS in empowerment.

This mythology of the religion is the most confounding and unbelievable to the modern people and is also a real source for orthodoxy. The variety of concepts of sheaths of JIVA, each relating to different corresponding LOKAS, make it difficult to conceptualize and believe. Science does not believe in the living energy or soul, as its sole concern so far has been material energy. In theology, the soul is regarded as an immaterial immortal and spiritual living entity, separable from the corporeal body at death, susceptible to happiness or misery in a future state. The concept of a soul in the religion is derived from the concept of JIVA, the living energy, as a subtle ANSHA of BRAHMAN, which goes through cycles of rebirths as explained earlier in subsection 2.2.3. This soul is described in this mythology as MANOMAYAKOSH, which carries empowerment through good or bad conduct in the previous birth. According to this empowerment achieved in the previous birth, the next cycle of rebirth and its associated happiness or misery or even moksha is determined.

A few cases of the resurrection of some human beings have been reported in some magazines and books. But no uniqueness is found in their narrations about what happened after their death. Therefore, all descriptions of what happens after death remain a myth. Science, of course, has discovered that some human organs such as the heart, kidneys, liver, etc., remain functional for a brief period after the brain death of a person, and these can be put on life support for a few days for the purpose of organ transplant to some other needy person. The mythological story of Lord GANESHA having a head transplant of an infant baby elephant also indicates the concept of organ transplant in ancient times. Thus, ancient knowledge as well as modern science both converge on the fact that JIVA or life remains active for a short while in the brain-dead corporeal body, and some organ transplant is possible, if needed. In the religion, only STHULA SHARIRA or ANNAMAYAKOSH is considered dead as a corporeal body. JIVA or soul remains in the SHUKSHMA SHARIRA or MANOMAYAKOSH for its onward journey to PRETLOKA. Only in case of very high empowerment, it quickly goes to SVARG. In case of low empowerment, JIVA remains in PRETLOKA for a longer period and then goes for suffering in NARAK. After spending its SVARG or NARAK period, JIVA either achieves moksha or returns for rebirth.

The concept of transition of the soul after death through PRETLOKA to NARAK or SVARG is the real source of orthodoxy propagated by the fraudster priests. They cheat the gullible relatives by demanding very high donations in the name of providing relief to the departed soul by making a quick transition from PRETLOKA and bypassing NARAK through certain worship rituals and donations. The concepts of soul, NARAK and SVARG are deeply embedded in the minds of the people for ages in almost all religions and cannot be easily wiped away through scientific and rationality preaching alone. It is the fear psychosis of the suffering ordeal in NARAK created by the fraudster priests for befooling the close relatives and demanding sometimes unbelievable donations for providing assurance of bypassing NARAK by the departed soul. This is an unethical practice on the part of the priests and is surely an orthodox that needs to be checked. People need to be educated by various religious societies and other religious congregations that the reward of NARAK or SVARG depends upon the good and bad conduct of the departed soul during his/her lifetime; this reward cannot be changed after death by any mantra or worship promised by any priest.

One may not subscribe to the concept of the various sheaths attached to the soul in its onward journey after death as enunciated in this tenet. However, the concept of awakened consciousness is thoroughly embedded in all religious and moral preaching for better and virtuous living and is also supported by many renowned scientists. The concept of awakening consciousness does not apply to the material energy pervading all through the universe. It refers to an awakening of the individual self, i.e., persona, which is full of passions, emotions and thoughts inside the material body. This is the live energy also called as soul in the religion. The religion believes that this soul carries quite a good deal of past life information, especially the rewards of good and bad conduct, to the next journey after death. The concepts of hell and heaven are quite in consonance with this belief so as to impress upon people the rewards of bad and good conduct in life after death. This creates a sort of fear psychosis in the minds of people against bad conduct. The fear psychosis does tame the wildness in the mind, at least to some extent if not wholly. But this fear psychosis should not be used by the priests for befooling the gullible close relatives of the departed soul. Various religious forums that are operating in every nook and corner these days must take this socio-religious work of educating the people on unchanging of the rewards of good and bad conduct after death, and also about how to counter the misguiding fraudster priests. There is an alternate theological philosophy that all rewards of good and bad conduct are received in the present life itself, and therefore, heaven and hell exist in this world only. If people are made to believe this alternate philosophy, then there would be no need to bother about the transition of a soul from one LOKA to another LOKA after death. If both the above ideas, i.e., (i) unchanging of rewards of good and bad conduct after death and (ii) rewards of good and bad conduct are received in the present life itself, are properly impressed upon the people through religious writings and preaching, then the reality and need for this most confounding myth can be totally eliminated in the religion without any loss of its religious intent and fervor.

2.3 GENERAL RELIGIOUS CUSTOMS AND RITES

Every religion prescribes several customs and rites to be performed by its followers. The Central Hindu College of Benares (1916) has identified a set of customs and rites to be performed by the followers of the Vedic Sanatan religion as also by other Hindu religions. These customs and rites are described in sections 2.3.1 to 2.3.7 to follow. The purpose of these customs and rites is to enable the empowerment of JIVA through a solemn, purposeful and virtuous life, and to seek benevolence from the Devas and Rishis. In the performance of these ceremonies, some material objects, gestures/postures and sounds are used in a carefully arranged manner. Objects like flowers, petals or fruits of a specific plant or tree, which help establish meditation and/or link the worshiper with the specific ISHWAR avatar or deity, are chosen for the performance of religious customs and rites. Gestures and postures, such as sitting in PADMASANA or standing with folded hands, help move the body and PRANA in a suitable way to have a calm and quiet mind for reverence. Postures activate potential energy and gestures activate kinetic energy. For example, the PADMASANA posture ensures that the entire body weight is put on the center of gravity of the body so that one can sit comfortably for long. Similarly, the clapping gesture during prayer does some acupressure on the palms, activating certain corresponding nodal points of the body for better energy flow. Sounds in the form of Bhajan or paean (hymn) are used to give rise to certain helpful soothing vibrations for creating steadiness of thought and devotion. Suitable sounds drive away hostile feelings/thoughts and negative energy, thus improving the surroundings of the place of worship. Mantras contain sounds in a definite succession, sequence and pitch for a specific purpose. The specific frequency and pitch of the sounds create the required vibrations, which define a particular mantra. The mantras need not be spoken aloud, and their silent repetition is, indeed, more powerful than audible recitation.

Religious ceremonies are considered sacred acts and need to be performed in a peaceful and fully devoted manner. The recommended material objects, gestures/postures and sounds help in creating a peaceful and devoted atmosphere for the participants and avoid any external distraction. In fact, the conduct of any activity with full concentration and devotion needs some sort of conducive atmosphere to avoid distraction of the mind and energy. Nowadays, people are using modern technological gadgets like loudspeakers, CD players, glaring lights and other decorations to make a ceremony more glamorous. This distracts the minds of the participants who then engage themselves more in unnecessary gossip than devoting themselves to the ceremonious rites and understanding their meaning and purpose. Then, the ceremonial rites simply become a formality to be conducted or participated in. This is how and why these ceremonies are now being regarded more as orthodox rituals. In fact, these ceremonies were planned and prescribed with some specific objective and purpose, according to which the procedure of conduct and rituals were stipulated, which must be followed by all attending the ceremony. Of course, these ceremonies also tend to serve as a get-together for the family and their acquaintances, but one must not lose sight of the main purpose of the ceremony. The simplicity, serenity and devotion make a religious ceremony properly solemnized with spirituality and divinity. Therefore, all technical gimmicks and glamorous presentations should be avoided to make the ceremony purposeful and achieve real spirituality and divinity.

2.3.1 Samskaras

There are ten main SAMSKARAS to be performed in the life of a person. Of these, seven relate to infantile life and early childhood. Of these seven, the sixth ANNAPRASANAM, the first feeding of the infant with solid food and the seventh CHUDAKARANAM or tonsure of the head and piercing of the ears are very common and generally practiced. The eighth SAMSKARA is UPANAYANA, which marks the student life with entire celibacy observance. After this stage, there is a formal return home the ninth SAMAKARA of SAMAVARTANAM. Then the tenth SAMSKARA of VIVAH, i.e., marriage, is performed, which marks the entry into manhood and its responsibilities as a GRIHASTHA. In modern days, the tenth SAMSKARA is not being followed properly and marriage is being forced without completing student life, which is a great disregard for the old Vedic Sanatan customs.

The religion prescribes a total of 16 Samskaras out of which 10 Samskaras are the main customs to be followed during a person's life. Of these 10, the first seven relate to the infantile and early childhood period of a person. The first five Samskaras relate more to keeping the mother and the infant in a peaceful and clean seclusion after birth for about 12 days, so as to protect them from any outside infection and harm through external exposure. During this period of 12 days, only simple worship and singing of pious songs and bhajans by the family members are done for the holy celebration of the birth of a child. The sixth Samskara relates to feeding the child with solid food after about six months, as till now the child was fed only the mother's milk. This is what modern scientific nutritional advice also promotes all mothers to do after the delivery of a child. The seventh Samskara relates to CHUDAKARANAM or tonsure of the head after one year. This tonsure of the head ensures a bountiful tuft of new hairs grown after the tonsure, which lasts for a much longer time and reduces the chance of baldness. Perhaps science has not experimented with this, but its practice since a long time and barbers' advice confirms its relevance. Otherwise also, periodical tonsure of the head is considered a good cleanliness practice that reduces the chances of fungal and other infections in the head.

The eighth Samskara relates to the UPANAYAN ceremony, which prepares the teen-aged child for the next phase of life that is to be devoted to studies and/or skill training, which would support his livelihood in the later period of life. During this period, also known as VIDYARTHY JEEVAN, i.e., student life, the child enters his youth, full of energy. So, the child is taught to observe certain rigorous practices of complete celibacy, hard discipline in daily chores, full devotion to studies and/or skill training, dutiful respect for teachers and other elders, and lead a compassionate and virtuous life. All this seems to be a good piece of wisdom. In fact, all modern schools, colleges and universities impress upon such rigors. The ninth Samskara relates to the successful end of studentship and return home, it is called SAMAVARTANAM. The tenth Samskara relates to the conduct of VIVAH, i.e., marriage, which marks entry into manhood and its responsibilities as a GRIHASTHA to perform other worldly functions.

All these Samskaras and their associated rites are good pieces of wisdom in preparing an infant to manhood for leading a righteous, compassionate and virtuous life as a responsible citizen of the society. The sixth Samskara of feeding the infant with solid food after six months is now recommended by doctors and nutritionists too and is mostly followed by all, though not with much ceremony. The seventh Samskara of CHUDAKARNAM is nowadays common only among the devout Sanatan families, but there is nothing orthodoxy about this for it prescribes periodic cleanliness of the head that protects it from fungal and other infections, and also gives a good tuft of new hair. The eighth and ninth Samskaras have drastically changed in modern times due to a new education system being followed in the country. Now the child is enrolled in school after attaining the age of five or even earlier. So, the eighth Samskara of UPANAYAN is generally not being practiced and is clubbed with the tenth Samskara of marriage as a pre-marriage ritual, and thus, has lost much of its sanctity. The ninth Samskara of SAMAVARTANAM is also not formally done as joining a job and settling into marriage have rendered it forgotten. In modern times, only the tenth Samskara of marriage is generally followed by all with great enthusiasm and glamor.

These Samskaras were devised and earlier practiced to train a young person on the protocols of the family and society, in terms of expressing one's response with etiquette, obedience and in an ethical manner, as also in the acquisition of creative and productive capabilities. The new education system has virtually forced the UPANAYAN Samskara to be postponed and followed merely as a ritual along with the marriage Samskara. Consequently, the virtues of a student life are now found missing during both the periods of preteens as well as teens. In fact, the age bracket of 5 to 20 years is a very sensitive period, full of curiosities and dreams in the most receptive young developing minds. That is why it is most suitable for education and training. But at the same time, these young minds should be warded off from all distractions that might allure them. The UPANAYAN Samskara aims to develop a state of mind, moral fear and willpower to help abstain from distractions and concentrate on righteous and virtuous living along with the acquisition of knowledge and training. This is what religious Samskaras aim to inculcate in the mind from childhood to adulthood.

But in modern times, most of the Samskaras are in wane and the institutions of joint families and relatives are also showing a decline. Therefore, the concepts of cohesive, compassionate and harmonious social structure are also disappearing. New concepts of modern life, nuclear family and even live-in relationships are in vogue. In the name of individual liberty and rights, individual pride, egoism, showoff, conceit, self-indulgence and indifference to others are becoming the characteristic features of modern life and its people. As a result, psychotic and psychopathic problems such as conflicts and fights, anxiety, stress, depression and even suicides have greatly increased, especially among young people. In the old days, when all these Samskaras were properly followed, joint family system, relatives and social groups were all fully functional as benevolent social institutions in the society. These social institutions, especially the joint families and relatives, used to work as the best psychotherapy centers that were easily available to a misguided, confused and betrayed person. These social institutions used to treat the person with full care, love and benedictions with no cost and no fee. With the social institutions in wane, persons having disturbed mental poise now rush to psychiatrists and hospitals for psychopathic treatment, which is not only costly but also involves a lot of trouble of running around. In fact, all the Samskaras were devised as good pieces of wisdom to keep the social structure fully functional and bring up the child as a responsible youth and adult. Thus, these Samskaras helped preserve the desired social environment that is now degrading. Therefore, all the Samskaras must be fully revived. There is nothing illogical or orthodoxy in these Samskaras.

2.3.2 Shraddha

SHRADDHA ceremonies are performed by family members and others, who remain in this world, to help the JIVA who has put off his visible body in death and is in PRETLOKA. After death, the ANNAMAYAKOSH, i.e., the physical body, is destroyed during cremation by burning it on a wooden pyre, but the PRANAMAYAKOSH is still retained by the JIVA as PRETA. SHRADDHA ceremonies help the JIVA peacefully transit from PRETLOKA to PITRILOKA and join other ancestors living in the subtler regions of BHUVARLOKA. When the JIVA finally reaches SVARGA, there is no need to help the JIVA by SHRADDHA ceremonies.

The SHRADDHA ceremony is conducted with a get-together of the family and other close acquaintances in order to show reverence and pay homage to the departed soul and other ancestors. This is a good and wise custom to pay homage to the departed soul and other ancestors as a mark of respect and grief for missing them. However, many people, including some saints and rationalists, have questioned the associated ritual of PIND DAN and the expenditure of money and materials used in a shraddha ceremony. The traditional shraddha ceremony involves three main rituals: one of PIND DAN to the departed soul; second of gifting the priest and other associated workers with some money and material in memory of the departed soul; and third of a parting feast with the family and acquaintances participating in the ceremony. The first ritual involves worship of the deities and the departed soul, and offering some simple food (mainly plain cooked rice) as PIND DAN to the soul only as a symbolic offering, and all food is later given to cows and birds (especially crows). Thus, there is no wastage of food. The second ritual, though expensive, constitutes a part of the traditional social security system of helping underprivileged people through some gifts and/or charity in socio-religious functions. In modern days, few individuals are compulsorily and substantially taxed in various ways to help the underprivileged through subsidies on various items such as ration, education, health care, etc., and it is termed as the social security system, which is often resented by those being taxed. In ancient days, the concept of social security was built up through donations, gifts and charities associated with various religious and socio-cultural ceremonies, and its expenditure amount depended upon the capacity of the individual conducting the ceremony, without any compulsion on the amount spent as gift and charity.

In ancient days, the priests generally lived an austere life with no other livelihood source except the donations and gifts received in religious ceremonies. They did not engage themselves in any other source of income and were trained only for the conduct of the Vedic religious ceremonies, for which they were held in high esteem and honored with gifts and donations. Then, a lot of arrangements were made, such as cleaning the place before and after the ceremony, arranging flowers, wooden stools and plantain leaves (both used for making a small temporary organic temple for placing idols for worship), earthen mugs and leafy plates for serving Prasad during the feast, etc. For all these arrangements and collection of materials, generally workers from the lower strata of society were engaged, who were very poor. Therefore, they were also given some material and money gifts and charity at the end of the ceremony. In this way, the ancient social security system took care of those less advantageous members of the society who did not possess any productive asset like land, an orchard, a shop, etc. and had no other source of income. The third ritual of a parting feast at the end is also expensive but the level of expenditure is not fixed and can be made variable to suit the capacity of the family conducting the shraddha ceremony.

The main objective of both the social security systems, modern and ancient, is the same—helping less advantageous and poor segments of society. The modern system is nowadays more admired for being nonconformist and rational, although it has the element of compulsion for all taxpayers and loopholes in its administration. Even this modern system of social security is resented by many people because of administrative loopholes in its administration. The ancient system had the element of variability on the extent of expenditure to be incurred on donation and charity depending upon the capacity of an individual. This helped maintain the social order in a non-market economy of the ancient days, and therefore, reflects the religion's concern in preserving the social milieu. However, it later became a source of orthodoxy due to some priests forcing the gullible relatives to make expensive donations to help transit the departed soul to Svarga. Later, the ARYA SAMAJ sect of the religion simplified these shraddha rituals by offering only a group prayer to ISHWAR with HAVAN and the Gayatri mantra, paying homage to the departed soul. All those who do not wish to follow the traditional ceremony can adopt the simplified ARYA SAMAJ way of conducting the shraddha/homage ceremony.

2.3.3 Shaucham/cleanliness

To ensure physical health and strength, rules for keeping bodily purity are prescribed under SHAUCHAM. There are minute-sized particles and microbes floating all around in the air and materials as well as on the body, which make the body impure. In addition, impure food like stale food and certain types of food like meat, egg, garlic, onion, etc., and impure air like the exhaled air containing obnoxious gases, also make the body impure and susceptible to diseases. Pure air and pure water along with fresh and clean food are essential for good health and strength. Therefore, the body must be built up with clean material and get thoroughly cleaned at least once every day. Parts of the body like hands and feet whenever soiled must be properly washed. Washing of hands before and after food must not be forgotten. We must be clean, not only for ourselves, but also for the sake of others. Above all, bad company and alcoholic drinks create impurity in the inner self, i.e., PRANAMAYAKOSH and MANOMAYAKOSH, hence must be avoided. The purity of MANOMAYAKOSH also depends upon the purity of desires and thoughts. All these constitute the guidelines for SHAUCHAM or cleanliness.

This rite puts great emphasis on the observance of cleanliness in our daily chores in order to ensure good physical health and strength. Stating that dust and microbes cause impurities all around, this rite suggests a daily bath, regular cleaning of soiled hands, eating fresh food, drinking pure water, avoiding certain tamas foods and drinks and also bad company. Thus, fairly all aspects of physical and inner cleanliness for healthy living are prescribed in this rite. Hence, this rite has a full scientific connotation. Modern science, through doctors, health workers and nutritionists, teaches people the various practices to be followed for healthy living and building physical strength. In modern days, these include regular health checkups, vaccinations, a nutritive diet and regular physical exercise. In the religion also, except vaccinations, which were not known in ancient times, all the practices are thought helpful for maintaining good health and strength and are recommended. The AYURVEDIC doctor called VAIDHYA provides all consultations, medical advice and treatment, if needed. In addition to outward physical cleanliness, inner bodily purity through good and fresh food, pure air, pure water and more than that good company are also emphasized for cleanliness and purity for not only the self but also for the sake of others. Therefore, this rite is highly scientific and full of wisdom.

2.3.4 The Five Daily Sacrifices

We all owe debt to our ancestors, devas and contemporary people who all have, directly or indirectly, shaped our existence in many ways. To pay this debt, the following five daily sacrifices are recommended.

(i) *Sacrifice to Rishis or Vedas by studying and teaching holy ancient scriptures. Every day, one should study some sacred book and acquire knowledge to understand oneself and duties. Also, one should share this knowledge with those more ignorant.*

(ii) *Sacrifice to Devas by conducting HAVAN in recognition of the providence of nature and its various elements, which are revered as Devas, with a pledge to live in harmony with nature.*

(iii) *Sacrifice to PITRIS by TARPAN, i.e., offering of water to ancestors for their sacrifices, which improved and enriched their posterity.*

(iv) *Sacrifice to Men by hospitality and helping humanity, particularly the less privileged people.*

(v) *Sacrifice to BHUTAS by putting a little food on the ground before beginning a meal for the invisible lower entities around us, and placing the remains of a meal in a suitable place for vagrant men and animals as a practice for kindness and consideration towards them.*

These five daily sacrifices aim to teach an individual that he is a part of a great whole and highlight the need for establishing harmonious relations with all – the past and present.

This rite emphasizes that one's performance and achievements as an individual would not have been possible without the role played and the base created for one's actions by others in the past and present. For example, if one is currently able to eat any fruit, it has been possible because someone else had planted a fruit tree in the past, and the payment of a price for the fruit is simply a current social practice to distinguish one as an entitled recipient. Similarly, without the language, script and diction developed by others in the past, one's present reading and writing would not have been possible with such an ease. The knowledge developed in the past, efforts of all the teachers, endeavors of parents and other family members as also that of so many other people who remained incognito, have all contributed, directly or indirectly, to one's present success and achievement. So, one should feel gratitude for the selfless gratuitous acts of others and offer some sacrifices for them through the rites prescribed for each group of people in the past and present. In fact, this rite makes one believe and understand that one is not an individual entity without others in society. One is just a part, however, presently important, of the whole system. This realization makes one shun all ego, pride and arrogance, and become humble and modest in dealing with others. As a result, this helps in reducing conflicts and fights and assists in making a cohesive, compassionate and harmonious society. Thus, this rite is full of wisdom in developing a harmonious social environment and making it sustainable in the long run.

2.3.5 Worship

Worship is the expression of love and reverence to the Supreme and aspiration to unite with HIM. It may be done in various forms such as praise of His perfection, appeal to His love, meditation on His Nature, and in many other forms according to the temperament and stage of evolution of the worshiper. For worship, some objects with attributes are needed, on which the mind can be fixed and emotions can be raised. SAGUN BRAHMAN is the object of worship, and whom all prayers and praise reach. Puja is a simple form of worship, done before an image or idol, mantra or prayer recited. UPASANA includes many forms of worship, including meditation and daily SANDHAYA and may require a qualified instructor for guidance.

This custom is the core of the religious practices and rituals. The object is to train the flickering and wandering mind to concentrate and focus on the Supreme, His love and care, and offer reverence to Him through worship. Worship can be performed in various manners, like many forms of PUJA or UPASANA. Worship can be done in a home or in a temple. As said earlier, the ancient theologians aimed to make the religion a way of life for the people. Worship is one way to achieve this objective. People are sermonized to do worship in many ways and on many occasions, such as in the morning and evening as a daily routine to offer reverence, during some ceremonies for its conduct without any hindrance or obstacles, prayer to solve or remove some problem being faced, prayer to help achieve or fulfill the desired objective, to console someone in the tragedy, etc. On all such occasions of worship, prayer and other rituals that are followed, fill up the hearts and minds of the worshipers with hope, poise and solace. During some worships, such as those conducted as a part of a daily routine and for problem-solving, children and other family members are also associated to inculcate the tradition of worship among them. This custom provides hope, poise and solace to the people and motivates them towards leading a righteous, virtuous and pious life; this is a desirable custom full of wisdom for developing a composed and helpful attitude among the people and building a compassionate society.

However, in the present times, the lack of real religious training, improper education, a rat race culture for modernity and consumerism, wicked competition in job and work, and neglect of family and social values are some of the reasons that have reduced the religious fervor greatly, building a selfish and uncaring attitude, especially among the young people. Their mental poise is quite disturbed because of severe despair in life, and some of them are becoming victims of several psychic disorders and psychosis like moral turpitude, desolation, depression, a tendency for suicide, etc. This is destroying the social fabric and charm of family and group living. The modern remedy for the brain fag and nervous exhaustion, of course, lies in medical and psychopathic treatments, though with a heavy cost and running around. But a simple act of worship, conducted with faith and belief in the supernatural power, reduces anxiety and tension, restoring the mental poise with some hope for betterment in life. Also, the earlier concept of joint family living with social attachment was the alternate remedy for treating despair in life without any heavy cost and running around. Simple family care provided solace and love, which served as a cure for mental agony. Thus, the custom of worship and prayer not only maintains the composure of an individual but also strengthens the joint family system and offers family-level psychic health care. Thus, in a way, worship and prayer help in preserving a better social ambiance.

2.3.6 The Four Ashramas

To regulate the wavering and fluctuating MANAH in the different stages of life, the Rishis marked out the plan for the life span between birth and death into four stages called the four ASHRAMAS. These four stages are: BRAHMCHARYA, the stage of studentship; GRAHASTHA, the stage of householder-ship; VANAPRASTHA, the stage of forest-dwelling, i.e., seclusion; and SANNYAS, the stage of total renunciation, i.e., asceticism. In any of these stages, one should not grasp the duty of the other three stages. Each stage has its own duties and its own pleasures, and these together lead to an orderly unfolding of the JIVATMA. The first ASHRAMA of life of student begins with the UPANAYANA ceremony and from that time forward certain virtues must be strived for. He must be strong, simple and chaste in thought and action, celibate in mind and body, industrious, obedient to teachers and seniors, and concentrate on his studies and/or training to develop knowledge and skill. The second ASHRAMA, that of the household stage starts with marriage, after completion of studies and/or training. This is the most important stage as it supports all the other stages. In this stage, one should acquire the qualities of a good husband/wife, a good father/mother, a good master and a good citizen. These qualities include unselfishness, compassion, tenderness, temperance, purity, helpfulness, prudence, industriousness, righteousness and charity. When the signs of age appear and children become able to bear the full burden of their responsibilities, both husband and wife should surrender the headship of home, and retire from active life and enter the third ASHRAMA for leading a quiet and secluded life, devoted to reading and study, philanthropy, counseling of youngsters. Finally, in very old age, one should enter the fourth ASHRAMA for leading a life of an ascetic and devoting to meditation and worship till death.

This custom advocates people to adopt and follow the way of life segmented in the four different ashrams, which in fact prescribe different lifestyles for different age brackets of life. The first ashram is of a student life, which normally begins at the start of preteens by performing the UPANAYAN samskara. Youth is full of tremendous energy that needs to be used for the development of a good personality, and the acquisition of knowledge and skill for creative and productive purposes in the next phase of life. The lifestyle and actions prescribed for a student's life aim to fulfill this objective. The student must be simple, strong and chaste in thought and action, celibate in mind and body, industrious, obedient to teachers and seniors, and concentrate on his studies or training. The second ashram begins after the student life ends and relates to the household age bracket. Here, the individual undergoes development into full manhood/womanhood, for sharing various roles in the family and society as well as for undertaking creative and productive ventures. For this, different lifestyle actions are prescribed so as to imbibe the required qualities for performing these roles of a good husband/wife, a good father/mother, a good master and a good citizen. The third ashram relates to the next age bracket—reaching senior citizenship—when the physical energy of the body starts depleting and rigidities in emotions and thoughts start appearing. The lifestyle for this ashram prescribes gradual retirement from active life and leading a quiet and secluded life devoted to study, philanthropy and counseling of youngsters. This helps in reducing the problems that arise due to a generation gap and helps in maintaining serenity and decorum in the family. The fourth and last ashram relates to very old age, when ascetic life with a bare minimum of food and other activities helps in leading a carefree and peaceful routine. This advocacy of leading life in four ashrams, each with defined separate lifestyles, aims at not only making one's life purposeful but also maintaining serenity and decorum in the family. This, in turn, strengthens the institution of joint family and society. So, this custom is full of logic and wisdom, and shows the religion's concern in sustaining the social environment in the long run in a harmonious and purposeful manner.

The routines prescribed for studentship in Brahmacharya ashram and Grahastha ashram are sufficient to absorb the mind and time in full. But the problem of full absorption of the mind and time is often felt in the third ashram of seclusion and the fourth ashram of renunciation. For peaceful and virtuous absorption of the mind, especially in old age, several alternatives exist, such as: going on a pilgrimage to holy places if physical health and finances permit, reading ancient sacred literature if literate with fine vision, joining a holy chorus at some nearby temple or holy congregation, teaching and training the younger generation on follow up of religious doctrine, practices and conveying the underlying logic and wisdom therein. Yoga and meditation can be combined with any of these alternatives. There are large numbers of holy places in the country and visiting these places would take an entire lifetime. Similarly, there are large numbers of ancient sacred literature – four VEDAS, 108 UPANISHADS and SMRYTI, and 18 PURANAS. Some contain knowledge and preaching, others contain interesting stories full of wisdom as well as worldly melodrama. Likewise, several temples have developed a holy chorus, starting from morning ARTI to various types of worship at different times of the day and also conduct discussions on different religious issues. A lot of holy congregations are periodically held, offering discourses on various religious matters. All these would not only be good enough for passing time but also perhaps better for mental poise and pious feelings rather than watching television for fictitious films and serials, YouTube presentations on the mobile or reading political gossip on social media. Thus, all these lifestyles described in the four ASHRAMAS seem to be quite full of wisdom in maintaining a calm, happy and purposeful environment in the family and society, which prevailed during the Vedic period.

However, nowadays, the concept of these four ashramas is losing significance and waning. The conduct and purpose of student life seem to have gotten lost in the modern system of education, wherein a child of 5 is forced to lose his charm of childhood and enter schooling, and grownup youth is falling into misapprehensions and misdemeanors rather than focusing on their studies and skill training. Those passing out successfully are becoming more of robots than being usefully creative and productive for society. In the second GRAHASTHA ashram, the husband and wife are generally running a rat race for money, luxury and their children's education rather than running a household. The people running in the third and fourth ashramas are generally not retiring to seclusion and renunciation, and are not giving up their rigidities and undue interferences in family matters in the name of their experience and achievements. The modern-day chaos witnessed in family and society, such as family feuds, family disintegration, nuclear family, misguided and disgruntled youth, etc., is the result of the waning of the system of the four ashramas of life. These chaotic results vouch for the logical and judicious approach prescribed in the customs and lifestyles of the four ashramas that are advocated in the religion. In fact, the religion does not merely give sermons on the reverence to ISHWARA and practices to be followed as a believer, but also prescribes dharma or duty as the way to making one's life purposeful with a contribution to strengthening the society. This shows the religion's concern for developing and sustaining the desired social ambiance in the long run. For group living of humans, the institutions of family and society are as important as quality education, liberty of thought and actions for material progress. If humans are to remain as humans, the institutions of family and society can help them remain so. Otherwise, material progress will not take much time to make them mechanical robots, all engaged in only a rat race.

2.3.7 The Four Castes

In the long journey of the JIVATMA, through its many births and deaths, when it acquires human life, there were four distinctly marked stages in the birth and death cycles as humans. These four stages were called as old VERNAS, recognized in the social polity as social castes. While passing through different births, the JIVATMA gradually empowered itself with the ability to perform different types of karmas. In the first stage, the young JIVA, having low empowerment developed obedience, patience and serviceableness and were born in the lower stratum of laborers, artisans, servants and manual workers of every kind. In the social polity such JIVATMAS were considered as born into the cast of SUDRAS. In the second stage, the JIVATMA grew up and empowered itself a bit more to develop an ability to organize labor and direct it, gain wealth, enjoy and use it, undertake greater responsibility and administer accumulated possessions, and were born in the commercial class of traders, industrialists, capitalists, bankers and managers of industrial concerns. In the social polity such JIVATMAS were considered as born into the caste of VAISHYAS. In the third stage, the JIVATMA grew further and empowered itself for wider responsibilities to legislate, rule, work unselfishly for the state and nation, use power to protect and regulate and not aggrandize itself, and were born in a higher stratum of kings, judges, legislators, warriors and keepers of order in the state. In the social polity such JIVATMAS were considered as born into the caste of KSHATRIYAS. In the fourth stage, the JIVATMA embraced the serene age, when earthly charms were not attractive, and it became a counselor, friend and helper, and was born in the class of priests, counselors, teachers of every kind, authors, scientists, poets and philosophers. In the social polity such JIVATMAS were considered as born into the caste of BRAHMANAS, the most empowered and unselfish ones who gave more to society and needed very little from them. They lived a very simple life devoted largely to religious and intellectual pursuits.

This was the social polity laid down by Manu, which worked well for many millenniums without any caste confusion or conflict. In this social polity the conduct of the person was indicative of his caste and not his birth or SAMSKARAS. Also, there was no concept of upper caste and lower caste. It was realized that everybody could not do well in all types of work. Some were good at doing mental work relating to reading, writing and discussing theological and philosophical matters and were called BRAHMANAS. Some were performing better in warfare and administrative controls and were called KSHATRIYAS. Similarly, some others were doing better in organizing production and trade and were called BANIYAS. Then, some people were not good at any of the above works and were engaged in miscellaneous petty menial works and were called SUDRAS. Thus, the conduct in the work done determined the caste of an individual. It was the empowerment and ability of the JIVATMA in certain types of conduct that was gained during the cycle of its previous birth and death, which determined the caste in which it was to be born next. In the ancient days, JIVATMAS at each stage of empowerment were born into bodies belonging to that stage of empowerment and ability, and the whole society was content and progressive.

But in modern days, VARNASANKARAS and caste confusion have come to the fore, as now, JIVATMAS at each stage of empowerment are being born into bodies of other stages of empowerment. Hence, disorder and disharmony have arisen in the society. Much of the evil arose due to people of each caste grasping the work of the other castes and thinking more of the rights of their caste rather than the duties it imposes. In fact, over time, the ancient caste system deteriorated due to foreign invasions and the resultant acculturation that took place through social mixing and imposition of several foreign systems of education, avocations and governance. The foreign governances dictated the status of certain groups of individuals and their responsibilities, depending upon their utility and commitment to the ruler, and rewarded them with better jobs and other perquisites. This elated the social status of certain groups of people. The foreign governance continued in the country for several centuries, almost during the past millennium. Because of the power and status granted by these rulers to certain groups of individuals, who in turn helped the foreigners continue ruling the country, the concept of higher caste and lower caste emerged as linked to birth in a particular caste family. The Vedic caste system was completely distorted. This gradually led to the exploitation of the lower caste people by those in the higher caste at the whims of power and status granted to the latter by the foreign rulers. Over time, this caste differentiation and exploitation gave rise to large-scale socio-economic inequalities and even to the untouchability of certain groups of people in the lower caste as they were forced to avocations of some very unhygienic work.

In fact, in the ancient Vedic period, the caste of SHUDRAS only denoted the people of the lower working class of village artisans, field workers, menial household workers, etc. In the ancient caste system, SHUDRAS were active and respectable partners in society, without any discrimination by the other castes. Only their lifestyle was simpler due to smaller earnings in manual and/or menial work, which they used to perform like that of the modern times' labor class. Similarly, in the ancient Vedic period, the BRAHMANAS used to devote themselves to only sacred religious activities and only received worship offerings made by the other caste people. In fact, BRAHMANAS in ancient times were living on a subsistence level, almost an ascetic life. But they were highly respected for their sacred knowledge and wisdom, and conduct of religious ceremonies, leading a simple ascetic life. The life of BRAHMANAS was almost an ordeal, learning all ancient scriptures for acquiring knowledge, conducting religious ceremonies and leading a pious ascetic life. Thus, the Vedic caste system, based exclusively on the conduct of the person, was entirely different from the modern caste system.

In present times, the caste system is denoted by the birth of a person in a particular family and everyone is doing the work and duty of one's own choice. In democratic governance of society, as presently followed in the country after gaining freedom from foreign rulers, an individual is allowed to pursue and adopt any avocation of choice if one's ability permits. Therefore, the ancient concept of caste linked to one's avocation/work performed does not hold any relevance in the present democratic setup of the country. Also, because of legal reservations in educational and job opportunities for lower and backward classes in the present times, the social hierarchy of higher caste and lower caste, developed during the foreign dominion period of the country, is also disappearing. Further, the feeling of nepotism, which is a general psychological weakness amongst all ethnic groups, is now developing more amongst the various caste fraternities. Therefore, the present caste system is now a complete misfit, having no significance in the present times of modern science and technology development. But the caste system has now acquired political patronage in the country due to the demographic strength of various caste groups, which is being considered as the social engineering in winning democratic elections. Several intellectuals and social reformers advocated for the abolition of the present caste system in the country because it has disturbed compassion and cohesion in the society through bickering among various caste groups. But it now quite suits the political game and maneuver that does not seem to favor its abolition.

The people themselves, if they feel so, have to take the initiative in abolishing the present caste system. The first very simple thing required to be done in this regard is to stop using surnames indicative of a particular caste on school certificates and onwards in life. Some people have already started doing so. This may, however, create a problem on how to distinguish between two or more individuals having the same name. One way would be to postfix either parent's name as the surname after one's own name so as to keep an individual's identity. This system is being followed in some southern states, where the father's name is added after one's own name. Nevertheless, these states are still overburdened with caste conflicts. Alternatively, one may postfix the village, town or city name as a surname. This is being practiced by some poets and writers and is also followed in some states in the southern region. Still, caste conflicts persist there too. Yet another alternative would be to postfix one's GOTRA of lineage as the surname, as is being done by some people. Despite all such alternatives being followed and practiced by many people, caste conflicts are still prevailing in the country, perhaps due to the present-day political exigency. To some extent, with varying flavor and fervor, the caste system prevails even in the highly rich and modern societies in several other countries of the world, which otherwise criticize the Indian caste system. In such countries, the caste system prevails de facto, though not de jure, on the basis of race, religion and regionalism. Therefore, the main issue of ensuring liberty, equality and fraternity among all citizens will always remain to be addressed by the governance of the country in modern times, whether the caste system flourishes or is abolished.

2.4 ARYA SAMAJ – VEDIC VARIANT

Around 500 BCE, several other religious philosophies emerged in the country, which contradicted the doctrine and tenets of the Vedic Sanatan religion. Among these, three major ones were CHARVAKA, JAINISM and BUDDHISM, which negated the Vedas and the existence of BRAHMAN or ISHWARA as the creator and governor of the universe, denouncing the concepts of reincarnation, soul and moksha. The CHARVAKA, also known as LOKAYATA, was founded by BRIHASPATI, and advocated atheism, heterodoxy and materialism to its followers. It believed in direct perception and rejected metaphysical and supernatural concepts like God, soul, reincarnation, moksha, etc. JAINISM was established by LORD MAHAVIR, who was the 24th and the last TIRTHANKARA of the religion. TIRTHANKARAS were born as human beings, attained enlightenment and were worshiped as gods by JAINS, who believe in rebirth, karma, virtuous living, non-possession, non-violence and nirvana. An erstwhile prince, Siddhartha, renounced his kingdom to become a sage, but later, after attaining enlightenment, is known as GAUTAM BUDDHA. His preaching led to the foundation of BUDDHISM, which also believes in rebirth, karma, virtuous living, non-possession, non-violence and nirvana. Thus, both JAINISM and BUDDHISM are quite similar in belief and practices, except that BUDDHISTS greatly revere GAUTAM BUDDHA but do not worship him as God. The concept of nirvana in both these religions simply refers to freedom from worldly miseries and rebirth, and is quite different from the concept of moksha in the Vedic Sanatan religion. In the 15th century AD, Guru Nanak Dev through his preaching, founded a faith quite distinct from Hinduism and Islam. Nine Gurus followed Guru Nanak and established the Sikh faith called Sikhism. Their holy book called the Guru Granth Sahib is a collection of 6000 poems of Sikh Gurus of the medieval period. Sikhs worship "WAHE GURU" as GOD who is formless, immortal and the creator of everything. Sikhism has three main tenets – devotion to the creator, trustfulness and service to humanity.

The emergence of the abovementioned theological philosophies around 500 BCE led to a war of nerves started by the followers of these philosophies with the Vedic Sanatan religion by greatly undervaluing its doctrine, tenets and rituals. This led to a general decline in the religious fervor for the Vedic Sanatan religion. In the ancient period, much of the Vedic knowledge was transmitted orally as shruti and remembered as smriti. With a decline in the intensity of the religious feeling and Vedic practices, some less competent and hypocritic priests, having poor smriti of the Vedas, took the central stage and started misconstructions of the Vedic mantras, rites and rituals in order to misguide and befool the gullible common people. The common man had little or no knowledge of the Vedic procedures for various religious ceremonies and depended on these priests. As a result, the religion was dominated by these fraudulent priests and gradually got debased. Many believers of the Vedic religion felt uncomfortable with these fraudster priests and started ignoring the Vedic customs and practices; some even adopted other philosophies, which were trying to play dominant roles in society.

In the eighth century, the great sage, Adi Shankaracharya, revived the Vedas and Vedic teachings in the country. He propagated the Advaita Vedanta philosophy, i.e., soul or atman is the same as BRAHMAN. Adi Shankaracharya traveled the length and breadth of the country on foot and established four Peethas (centers) for Vedic teaching and practices – one each at Sringeri Sharda Peetham in Chikamanglur, Karnataka; Govardhan Peetha in Puri, Orrisa; Sharda Peetha in Dwarika, Gujarat; and Jyotir Peetha in Joshimuth Badrinath, Uttarakhand. In addition, the Kanchi Mutt near Chennai was his abode and a great center for his Vedic preaching and practices. After him, two more Vedic scholars made prominent contributions through their commentaries on the Vedas, Upanishads and Brahma Sutras. One, sage Ramanujacharya, in around the 11th-12th century, propagated the Vishishtadvaita philosophy, which believes that BRAHMAN, as qualified in sentient (awareness) and insentient modes, is the only reality. Another, sage Madhavacharya, in around the 13th century, propagated Dwaitvad, which believes that the soul depends on BRAHMAN, but is never identical; both are unchanging realities.

In the 19th century, two great socio-religious reforms were initiated in the country, one by Raja Ram Mohan Roy by establishing the Brahmo Samaj in the year 1828 in Kolkata, and another by Swami Dayanand Saraswati by establishing the Arya Samaj in the year 1875 in Bombay, now Mumbai. Both these movements worked to eradicate the then prevalent evil practices of sati tradition, child marriage and polygamy, which evolved through fraudster priests during various Muslim rules. Both these reformers also promoted women's education, equal status to all in the society and a sense of national consciousness among the people. Brahmo Samaj was a reformist with a peaceful approach and supported the western culture. Therefore, it appealed more to the intellectual people. The Arya Samaj was more aggressive, supported the Vedic culture and rejected the western culture. Hence, it made better appeal to both educated and uneducated people. The Arya Samaj was established as a modified and reformed variant of the Vedic Sanatan religion with a view to reestablish the Vedas and modify the distorted practices that had been introduced in the religion through the fraudster priests during the long period of Muslim rules, which in fact led to the adoption of the sati tradition and child marriage to escape tortures on widows and the girl child.

Swami Dayanand Saraswati wrote several books, some of which are commentaries on the Vedas while others describe in detail the conduct of various Vedic rites and ceremonies. One of his books, written in 1875, entitled "SATYARTH PRAKASH" has become a household name among the followers of Arya Samaj. The book expounds on various issues relating to the conduct of life in the four Vedic Ashramas, virtuous living, evolution of the world and commentaries on the various other sects of Hindu religion as well as on Christianity and Islam. Most of his writings were in the Sanskrit language, some of which were translated into English by others. He aimed to reestablish Vedic knowledge and started great social reform against the then prevalent socio-religious evil practices in the society, e.g., distorted caste system based on birth in a family, child marriage, restrictions on women reading the Vedas, the sati tradition for widows, etc. Swami Dayanand Saraswati greatly admired the work of the great sage Adi Shankaracharya of the eighth century, who revived the Vedas and propagated the Advaita Vedanta philosophy. Swami Dayanand Saraswati established the Arya Samaj to start social reforms through Vedic culture because of his belief in the infallibility of the Vedas and the supremacy of the Aryan culture.

He strongly denounced many customs and rituals that were developed and practiced during Muslim rule in the country. The most important among these denouncements was of sati burning. He also supported the re-marriage of a widow as NIYOG with another close relative for the production of a child to the family of the deceased. He also denounced the shraddha ceremony and advocated for a simple homage-paying ceremony with Gayatri Mantra and HAVAN, done on the third or fourth day after death. He criticized child marriage and suggested a separate marriageable age for boys and girls based upon their completion of education and puberty crossing level. He criticized idolatry and incarnations of ISHWARA as propagated in various Puranas and believed in only NIRGUN ISHWARA as being true Vedic knowledge. He strongly advocated the importance of education for girls to make them better mothers and home managers. He also advocated for a vegetarian diet and denounced the tradition of sacrificing animals after the HAVAN ceremony. He considered HAVAN very pious and necessary for cleaning the air and atmosphere. He suggested the recitation of the Gayatri Mantra to be followed by HAVAN as good worship practice for the people. Influenced by his book and preaching, many people adopted the Arya Samaj practices as a part of the Vedic religion.

CHAPTER

SOCIO-RELIGIOUS CUSTOMS 03

3.1 TRADITIONAL VERSUS MODERN

In ancient times, several socio-religious customs were developed in order to promote a way of life with religious orientation, social harmony and preservation of the natural resource base. These customs were practiced and passed on from generation to generation as traditions and became a part of what is now called a traditional lifestyle. A lot of people, especially in small towns and rural areas, still lead the traditional way of living and follow the traditional socio-religious customs. With developments in the modern education system, especially for higher and professional education, and the emergence of a technology-dependent work culture, many people have changed their way of living to what is now termed as the modern lifestyle, which is mostly copying the lifestyle of western countries. These changes often lead to a war of nerves between the traditionalists and modernists due to some misconceptions held by the latter, doubting the scientific rationality and wisdom in the socio-religious customs of the religion.

In fact, the war of nerves between the traditional and the modern was initiated by Thomas Macaulay, a British educationist, by introducing a new English medium education system in 1835 in BRITISH INDIA to teach subjects like English, Mathematics and Science to Indian students. This, in fact, intended and successfully achieved the enslavement of the Indian mentality by dividing the people into two cultures of backward traditional versus modern scientific—the latter was to support and help the British Empire. This education system, by and large, made students literate snobs to exercise command over others. This newly educated class of people was regarded as modern, having a scientific temperament and rationality, and was given all the privileges of power and modern living. People with traditional living were debased and considered as a lower rung in society. The modern educated young minds were made to believe that modern living inspires growth and development while traditional living hinders growth and development.

This clever ploy not only served to rule the country through modernists, but also served well in exploiting the local resources through cheap traditional labor to produce raw material and ship the same to support the then ongoing industrial revolution in England during the 18th and 19th centuries. The war of nerves between the modernists and traditionalists further escalated after the independence of the country in 1947, because the education system, by and large, remained the same except for growth in the number of such educational institutions. The demand for educated modernists kept rising with planned development and growth strategies adopted in the subsequent five-year plans.

After independence, the modern concepts of secular democratic governance, social justice, human rights and planned socio-economic development have been adopted in the country. Accordingly, constitutional provisions, legislations, civil charter and penal codes, development machinery and infrastructures have been planned and put in operation for compliance. This is termed as the most rational, civilized and modern approach of governance and development. But the development agenda, by and large, is rarely prepared in consonance with the socio-cultural milieu and the degrading natural resource base of the country. In the name of modernization, some development programs, either copied from other developed countries or urged by the lure of large investments from some multinational companies, are rushed up. These modernization programs have led to the hazards of pollution, energy crises and degradation of natural resource base, along with several other environmental problems. Then remedial measures are rushed up, which again lead to even more such problems. The rat race for modernization continues to adversely affect the natural environment, social ambiance as well as mental poise and health of the individuals trapped in this race.

In ancient times, the development agenda was fully in consonance with the local conditions, especially the social milieu and the resource base. This greatly helped in the preservation of the social environment as well as the natural environment. The values of simple living and contentment, conservation of resources through repair and reuse, love and respect for family and social relations, concern and attention to the local ecosystem, devotion to religion and the associated dharma (duty) were imbibed in the human mind through socio-religious practices. Civil behavior was ensured through religious and socio-religious practices infused in the mind right from childhood to the final cremation. The awe of ISHWARA and social disgrace/boycott acted as two great socio-religious deterrents to human ill-manner and wildness. Disputes, when arose, were resolved in the local panchayat or by mutual settlement through relatives and close inhabitants. Simple living included eating vegetarian food, doing most of the work manually, repairing machines and tools, recycling and reuse of materials in order to conserve resources and energy and leading a truthful life without pretensions or fancy shows. All these constitute the traditional lifestyle, which is still being followed by a large majority of people, especially in small cities and villages.

In traditional living, people follow conventional lifestyles in food, clothes and home management, and pass their time in entertainment through folk songs, traditional games, religious worship, singing prayers, reading sacred books and discussing various incarnations of ISHWARA and other deities, without any harm to the ecosystem or creating an energy crisis. Values of contentment and kindness are inculcated into human behavior along with actions to drive away greed and envy. This simple and virtuous living in the ancient past helped achieve high growth and development in both spiritual and material progress as revealed by several ancient foreign visitors to India, such as Fa-Hien, Hiuen-Tsang, Ibn Battuta, Al Baruni, Marco Polo, etc. It was this high growth and development that tempted many rulers from mid-Asian and European kingdoms to invade and loot the country.

In modern living, the concepts of family and a cohesive and harmonious society have virtually disappeared. Friendships and social clubs are generally formed as mutually convenient groups. The social disgrace/boycott and the awe of ISHWARA have even lost their significance, much less being a deterrent for human ill-behavior and wildness. In the name of individual liberty and rights, the social norms and harmony have virtually become a casualty. As a result, individual likings, pretensions and showbiz, and the indiscriminate use of technology often cross the line of decency and even legal limits to become a serious problem and discomfort to other people. In addition, there is no concept of resource conservation in modern living because the use-and-throw culture is more fashionable and widely prevalent. This may lead to faster linear growth in the economy, but it also leads to wastefulness in the use of electricity, and metallurgical and synthetic materials, contributing to pollution, resource depletion and unmanageable waste disposal problems.

In modern living, people copy the western lifestyle in food, clothes and home management, and pass their time in entertainment through film and television shows, mobile games and chats, and gossiping about film or sports celebrities or politics. For this, they add on a lot of technological gadgets, which soon become pieces of junk, spoiling the ecosystem and creating an unmanageable e-waste disposal problem. In fact, the very concept of modernity is based on the craze of becoming nontraditional. But in the process, modernists follow the traditions of the western countries. To illustrate, due to near-freezing temperatures and the non-availability of normal water in some western countries for over six months in a year, people there customarily use paper napkins and tissue paper instead of water for cleaning their hands, mouth and anus. The modernists here are imitating their tradition with a sense of modernity despite fair temperatures and easy availability of normal water in the country; and the fact that paper can never do the scientific cleaning that water can.

As for the scientific temperament, the so-called most modern and civilized societies all over the world, as also in the country, are raising and killing farm animals for their food, which is the same as the backward tribals hunting and killing animals for food. Advanced civilization must be based on compassion for all living beings. Even elementary scientific investigation brings out the fact that first growing feed for farm animals, then feeding, raising and killing animals and then processing their meat for human consumption is much more costly and highly energy-consuming as compared to growing food crops and processing these for direct human consumption. Recent research has shown that plant protein is superior to animal protein. Even the much hyper-emphasized campaign on stopping cruelty towards animals has miserably failed to stop the killing of animals for food. Furthermore, on scientific temper, the science and technology-based modern lifestyle has raised the energy demand tremendously, turning it into a big energy crisis. The fossil fuel burnt for transport and electricity generation has caused much physical damage to the natural resource base of land, water and air, leading to large-scale pollution that causes serious health hazards like rising incidences of cancer, TB and heart attacks. It also leads to severe environmental degradation and climate change problems. More than that, despite full awareness of these adverse happenings, the charm of careless luxurious living is so hypnotizing that nobody is willing to initiate even very small steps on energy saving in their own daily life by simply reducing the uncared wasteful usage of electricity and fossil fuels through careful planning and implementation of their daily activities.

In fact, the concept of traditional living has not been properly evaluated, instead, it has been debased as unscientific and orthodox living. It hardly matters whether one wears a western dress or a local traditional dress, whether one sings a filmy song or a folk song and religious prayer, whether one worships a modern celebrity from politics/sports/film line or a religious celebrity. One could as well be a copycat of western countries or an original model of own country. It is all a matter of an individual's choice and liking, nothing of the sort being modern or traditional. But it does become a matter of serious concern if it generates some sort of superiority or inferiority complex among the people with respect to their lifestyles and the consequent repercussions on human creativity and social well-being. With the observations and facts stated above, this chapter examines the science and wisdom in some socio-religious customs that are usually followed in traditional living.

3.2 SOCIO-RELIGIOUS CUSTOMS

3.2.1 Multitude of Deities

Nature occupies the most important place in the Vedic Sanatan religion, which has protection of nature as one of its cardinal mandates. Nature, through its ecosystem, provides the basic elements for the existence and survival of life. Hence, nature is sanctified, revered and protected through various socio-religious ceremonies prescribed in the religion. The ancient Vedic epics describe all the elements of nature such as water, air, fire/energy, earth and other planets as DEVATA, i.e., the generous benevolent, because they offer the basics of life and survival without even asking. So, all these elements of nature are accorded the status of deities to be revered and worshiped by the people. The ancient theologians thought that in this way, people would express their gratitude and would not even dream of the degeneration or destruction of these elements of nature personified as different deities. To develop and enforce faithful social awareness of the importance and preservation of nature and the environment in religion constitutes a very important philosophical approach of the ancient Vedic Sanatan religion.

For example, newlywed ladies in the religion are taken to nearby wells and ponds to offer reverence and worship these water sources so that they could understand the importance of preserving water in wells and ponds. People conduct the puja ceremony with HAVAN (burning fragrant incense materials on firewood in a specific earthen vessel) after the successful completion of some religious celebration to offer reverence and worship to air, fire, earth and the other nine planets of our solar system, and infuse a sense of their being sacred deities having providence for sustenance and survival of all living creation. Likewise, both small and large elements of the ecosystem like ants, snakes, cats, dogs, cows, elephants, etc., are also protected and preserved by offering food to them on certain festive occasions. This inculcates the concept of diversity in the ecosystem in partnership with human living, as well as the virtue of non-violence and compassion. In the same way, there are so many other religious ceremonies for reverence and worship of a large number of deities incorporated from nature.

In the Vedic Sanatan religion, there are three SAKAR revelations of ISHWARA in the form of the trinity avatars of VISHNU, SHIVA and BRAHMA. They are revered and worshiped, and each of them is called as BHAGWAN. Then, there are three of their respective consorts named LAXMI, PARVATI and SAVITRI, also revered and worshiped. Further, PARVATI also has revelations as nine forms of Mother DURGA, depicting the various types of female Shakti or power, such as love, care, power, compassion, protection, etc. These nine forms of PARVATI are worshiped twice every year as Navratri for nine days. Out of the ten incarnations of VISHNU, depicting mythology of the evolution on earth, two incarnations are in the form of RAMA and KRISHNA, representing respectively the evolution of an ideal and complete human personality, are deeply revered and worshiped especially on their respective birth anniversaries. These are all the Gods and Goddesses revered and worshiped as major deities. Then GANESH, son of SHIVA and PARVATI, is worshiped as a very powerful deity for prosperity, the blissful start of any venture/activity and protection from troubles. Also, HANUMAN, a devout of RAMA, is considered a very powerful deity for protection from all evils and deliverance in all missions. These are the most revered and worshiped deities. Then there are five major elements of nature whose respective lords are worshiped in various ceremonies for their providences, e.g., Indra for water, Varun for air, Agni for fire, Prithvi for mother earth and Aakash for cosmic powers. Further, nine planets of our solar system are also revered and worshiped as the 'Nau Graha' on all major socio-religious ceremonies: these are the Sun, Moon, Mars, Mercury, Jupiter, Venus, Saturn, Rahu and Ketu (the last two being shadow planets conceptualized by the ancient rishis in Indian astrology – Rahu for material wealth and Ketu for spiritual vibrations). This makes quite a large multitude of deities, each specialized for some specific type of divine care and prayer.

In addition, rivers and mountains, in general, and some specific places, trees, animals and insects are also considered sacred and are revered, some even worshiped on special occasions. Thus, the religion advocates and practices the concept of harmonious living in the ecosystem. For example, rivers, in general, are considered sacred, and hence, respected. But some rivers like the Ganga, Yamuna, Narmada, Kaveri and Godawari are worshiped by the local populace on specific occasions. Likewise, mountains, in general, are considered sacred. But some mountains such as the Kailash and Himalayas are especially worshiped. Similarly, some local places on account of being the place of birth or samadhi of some famous saint/sufi fakeer are also revered and worshiped. Further, some especial trees like banyan, pipal, neem, mango and banana are also considered holy and are revered. The banyan and pipal trees (both fig trees) are even worshiped in some special religious ceremonies, e.g., the banyan tree in the Karva Chauth festival and the pipal in shraddha ceremonies. Both these trees offer many benefits to the people and are known for their medicinal values, being good for the environment in terms of foliage and providing good shade and shelter to birds and animals almost throughout the year. The neem tree possesses strong antibiotic properties and cleans the air, and is, therefore, revered. The leaves/branches and fruits of the mango and banana trees are considered holy and used in almost every religious ceremony. Mango wood stools and banana leaves are used for quickly making a temporary temple for worship anywhere anytime and can be easily disposed of. Small branches of the mango tree are used for burning firewood during a Havan ceremony. Mango and banana fruits are used as holy offerings for deities and later for distributing the same as holy Prasada (divine blessing) to the people participating in the ceremony. In the same manner, domesticated animals like cows for milk, cats for rat control and dogs as watchdogs, ants as small scavengers, snakes for control of other reptiles and small animals, sparrows for control of insects are also revered.

It may be beyond the perception and comprehension of the modernists and rationalists who criticize the worship of deities and various elements of nature, calling them unscientific and orthodox rituals. But no other institution in the so-called modern scientific and civilized world, including the various international forums under the United Nations, has so far succeeded in evolving and enforcing such a faithful awareness and concern towards the environment and ecosystem among the people. The Vedic Sanatan religion did so very successfully through several socio-religious customs and traditions, which really served so well in protecting the environment as well as the social fabric for millenniums, until recently when these customs and traditions started getting waned due to modernism. The worship of a multitude of deities and various elements of nature did create a psyche of reverence in society. It is a matter of simple psyche that people would not destroy or harm any element of nature that they revere and worship. This psyche served very well to protect the environment as well as the social structure in the past. Therefore, reverence and worship of a multitude of deities as also the elements of nature are fully scientific and rational as these worships help protect both the natural and social environments.

3.2.2 Murtipuja (idolatry)

Humans are said to be more social than other animals. For proper functioning of any social system, the norms of virtuous, compassionate and cohesive living must be inculcated among the people right from their childhood and young age. This is achieved through cultural orientation done by different people at different times and in different places like homes, schools, temples, etc. In the Vedic Sanatan religion, regular worship of the different avatars of ISHWAR and other deities in homes and temples was introduced for both religious as well as cultural orientations. Paying reverence and doing worship not only brings peace and solace to the human mind, but also provides cultural orientation through intermittent discourses on the life and achievements of the various avatars and deities and other religious celebrities, which motivates people for righteous and cohesive living. Cultural orientation cannot be properly infused only through abstract sermons and speeches. Stories of some special laudable performances and excellent achievements of some role models serve as motivating examples to be followed and possibly replicated by others. While abstract sermons and speeches may disappear from the mind after some time, good stories of some role model examples stay in the memory and continue motivating and inspiring the mind for follow-up in life.

Since ancient times, the stories of various avatars and other deities have served as a source of motivation, especially for young minds to follow up on their examples. The narration of any story becomes more purposeful, appealing and absorbing if done before any murti or idol personifying the concerned avatar or deity or role model. It helps in easily relating the laudable special performance to the specific performer in the minds of the listeners-cum-viewers. It sort of becomes an audio-visual presentation, which has a far better impact as compared to a simple audio presentation. It is quite a normal human psyche to recall a specific performance just by seeing the figure or murti of the performer. People carry in their minds the moral of the story embodied in the murti or idol. Particularly the young minds get fully engrossed in the story personified in the murti or idol. This is how and why murti/idol puja or idolatry of so many avatars and deities evolved in the Vedic Sanatan religion. There is nothing backward, illogical and unscientific about this evolution, rather it is a perfectly human psychological phenomenon.

Even in recent times, the fanciful and fictitious stories of Harry Potter, Batman, Spiderman, etc., have broken all records of popularity and publication in the so-called most modern, scientific and logical western world. These stories have even been translated into several languages and have very well spread to other countries, including India. Further, full movies and illustrated pictures of characters performing in these fictitious stories have been published and circulated all over the world. Young children in the modern world even invoke and implore these characters as role models to help them in crisis and difficulty. These modern time stories have amazed not only kids and young minds but also grownups all over the world. No one has dared to call these fictitious stories and their impact on children's psychology as illogical, unscientific or orthodox. Then how come Indian mythological stories and idols are leveled as tribal, unscientific and orthodox? This depicts not only biases but also snobbery in the minds of the critics.

For worship purposes, any murti or idol is first solemnized and consecrated by the pious act that involves sacred rituals and recitation of special mantras by an accomplished and trained priest. After this consecration, the murti does not simply remain some stone carving or painting, but it represents a sacred embodiment of the energy of the specific avatar or deity, thereby possessing the power of giving blessings and hope for success to its worshipers. Reverence and worship represent a feeling of profound respect and obeisance. The worship of a murti of SAGUN ISHWARA or any other deity as a part of reverence, reinforces the faith and trust of the believer. In the Vedic Sanatan religion, different incarnations of ISHWARA have been conceptualized in addition to a large number of other deities, each representing a particular domain of providence and/or energy. This makes these incarnations and deities specialized for different mundane requests, for example, VISHNU and LAKSHMI for management and wealth, SHIVA and PARVATI for meditation and energy, GANESHA for prosperity and hurdle-free compliance in any work, HANUMAN for physical power and protection from evil forces, etc. The worship of NIRAKAR ISHWARA was generally done by rishis and saints for the abstract purpose of seeking special empowerment for renouncing the world and seeking Moksha.

To make worship a ceremony, a set of paraphernalia was prescribed, like placing the murti or idol at some suitable place of worship, representing a symbolic or complete temple, doing ARTI with a flaming lamp, singing paean/BHAJAN in praise of the avatar or deity, touching the idol's feet, and offering some flowers and sweets to the idol to be later accepted and distributed as Prasad (divine blessing) among the participants. Worship of the idol creates a sense of attachment with and belonging to the ISHWARA or deity, which is present before the worshipers embodied in the murti or idol. People feel solace and happiness after performing worship. It is a very simple psychological fact that an object makes concentration better, develops a sense of belonging and remains in memory for long. Without an object, the mind flickers in the whirlpool of thoughts making concentration difficult. The idol personifies an image of the ISHWARA or deity visualized in the mind. The idol is consecrated and made sacrosanct by pronouncing sacred mantras and doing ARTI with a flaming lamp to offer fire energy to the idol. This establishes the idol as sacred and holy for daily worship. Thus, worship of the idol or murti puja helps in the concentration of the mind for a while, as it stays detached from other daily routine matters, providing relaxation and solace to perplexed minds. It is normally made part of a daily routine in the morning and/or evening. To call it a pastime will be an undue simplification but it sure is made to be a way of life for the common people.

Some modern people criticize murti puja as a waste of time and a creation of servitude to the deity in the minds of the people. After all, what do modern people normally do nowadays in their free time in the morning and evening? Either they watch WhatsApp/Facebook/YouTube on their mobiles or play games on mobiles/computers or watch some television show/film or simply chatter. They may feel happiness in this way of spending leisure time. But this way of life makes them more of an addict and servile to technology with excessive dependence on it. This is not only highly energy-consuming but also requires more money. In this way of life, people loosen their attachment to ISHWARA and the religion, and become self-centric, technology-servile and egoistic. These changes are seen nowadays in human attitude and behavior, distorting the whole social fabric and giving rise to a new set of socio-cultural complexities. Social harmony is disturbed due to the failure of mutual adjustment and cohesiveness. As a result, the psycho-therapeutic institutions of family and social relationships are losing significance and relevance, and psycho-medico cases of nervous exhaustion, depression, drug addiction and even suicidal tendencies are increasing. Technology is no doubt very helpful and provides great satisfaction in performing some work, but it also makes people more and more technology servile, always running after technological innovations and losing contentment and peace of mind. Such a scenario is quite visible nowadays with people who are increasingly adopting a technology-addict culture and losing their mental poise and peace.

However, despite all divine goodness, murti puja or idolatry has lost its purity and sanctity nowadays and has become almost orthodox. In most cases, it has become a ritual that is performed solely for the show of being a religious and spiritual person. A good deal of modern paraphernalia, like filmy BHAJANS, are played on loudspeakers that create jarring noise pollution and are a disturbance to others, particularly sick persons and students. Also, big advertising banners about the puja are put up, wasting a lot of cloth and paper that could be put to better use. Stalls for Prasad distribution to general people are being set up without hygiene and sanitation arrangements. A lot of floral decorations and many other things have been added in both private and temple puja ceremonies. In fact, floral decorations of the scenario and floral offerings to the murti as well as Prasad distribution create more problems of hygiene and sanitation rather than beauty and reverence or charity, especially in temples and public places. Those temples and other worship places where these practices are absent look very neat and clean and are a peaceful sanctum, depicting a more serene and pious atmosphere. Let flowers remain beautiful on plants/trees; follow the old saying that beauty is to see and not to touch. Similarly, let Prasad material be saved for those hungry who often sleep without food. Let us preserve the sanctity of murti puja as a devotional ceremony and not make it a theatre-like pomp and show. A place of worship is a sanctum sanctorum and not for ostentation. Without the true elements of piousness, sanctity and serenity, as being seen nowadays, murti puja becomes not only an orthodox but also a nuisance to those not participating in it. Therefore, the sanctity of the murti puja must be restored by simplicity, serenity and piousness to make it purposeful, as explained earlier. Priests and other holy persons participating in such ceremonies must ensure that it is done in a holy manner.

Further, the pictures of some avatars and deities are being printed on anything meant for sale or promotion in order to solicit the attention of the people with a touch of divinity, but without doing any act of consecration and solemnization. In some cases, even the names of some avatars or deities are used as the brand name, pictured and printed on the wrappers and/or containers. Later, these wrappers, containers and other printed materials are carelessly thrown here and there as waste, creating unceremonious indignity, disregard and an act of blasphemy to the avatar and deity printed on the paper or cloth. This is an unscrupulous and immoral act, which makes others call murti puja illogical and orthodox. This is against the religious Dharma and should be resented by everyone by boycotting such items in purchase and use. It is to be reemphasized that without proper consecration and solemnization, any murti or idol remains simply a picture or piece of clay, having no divine and blessing power. The use of any murti or idol of some deity for advertisement is an act of disregard and blasphemy, which should be resented and boycotted by every religious person.

3.2.3 Power of Mantra and Prayer

Energy is the capacity to do work. It is available in various forms such as light, heat, sound, electrical, chemical, nuclear, etc. Sound energy moves in the form of quanta waves, having a specific pitch and frequency (cycles per second). Sound waves in the frequency range of 20 Hz and 20,000 Hz, i.e., cycles per second, are audible to a human's hearing organs. Ultrasound waves have a frequency above this audible range. Every material has a specific frequency and by creating this frequency the material can be vibrated. In the year 1831, a suspension bridge called the great Menai Bridge on the river Irwell near Manchester, England, collapsed with the sound of the march-past steps of the soldiers. This sound created a frequency equal to that of the combined materials of the bridge. Therefore, it vibrated and collapsed. After this incident, it was made a general rule in the military to break the steps of the soldiers while crossing a bridge. This shows the power of sound energy, which could also be harnessed for useful purposes. In modern times, the power of sound energy is being harnessed in various ways such as radio waves, microwaves, ultrasound, etc., in communication and healthcare industries.

The ancient rishis of India had also realized the power of sound energy and developed various mantras embodying sound energy for various purposes such as: (i) prayer mantras for doing general worship or specific worship of ISHWARA and other deities for the fulfillment of some specific objective, (ii) welfare mantras for offering specific blessings or general well-being and healing of mind or body ailments, (iii) siddha mantras such as for deep meditation and Samadhi to reach a union with ISHWARA or do other mystic acts of HUTTHA yoga. Each mantra has some specific words arranged, as a hymn, to be chanted in a particular pitch and specified frequency. Therefore, each mantra is loaded with energy waves in terms of the specified pitch and specified frequency of sound. The words as such may have little significance in just relating a mantra to a particular deity and objective or purpose. It is the specified frequency and pitch of the sound of a mantra that matters in creating the desired effect. For example, some frequencies of sound can irritate the mind, e.g., loudness, while some others can soothe the mind like a sweet melody. Thus, some mantras may have the power to soothe an irritated or depressed mind. Likewise, some mantras may have the power to produce heat on spasmodic muscles and heal them like doctors do with modern sonic tools. Similarly, some mantras may have the power to clear obstacles in the way, like a fallen boulder, by rolling it over by matching with its frequency (like the case of a collapsed bridge mentioned earlier).

In any mantra, the power lies in the energy of the sound waves associated with its pronunciation and chanting, and not simply in the words used. Without the associated sound frequency and pitch, the words remain just spoken text. Thus, the power of mantras is the power of the associated sound waves. In that sense, mantras also relate to different music ragas that specify different scales of pitch and frequency. So, each mantra is to be chanted in a specific music raga. Each raga has its special feature in terms of the musical scale/meter, a suitable time for singing and the purpose of singing, such as in a general concert or to create a special effect. For example, during war time, poetic recitations in special VEER RUS raga are used to raise the tempo among fighting soldiers. In a king's court and other concerts, generally soothing and relaxing ragas, according to the time of the concert, are used. There are stories about some highly accomplished saints who sang the DEEPAK RAGA to burn a lamp, while some saints sang the MEGHA RAGA to make clouds rain. Contemporary musicians vouch for the reality of the existence of such ragas, though these are very difficult to learn and practice. In modern times, television serials like the RAMAYANA and MAHABHARATA use the signal tunes at the start of these serials in a special raga to arouse a feeling of divine reverence and worship in the minds of the viewers. All these examples indicate the power of sound to create some special desired effect, which is the core of any mantra and not just the spoken words. Proper recitation of any mantra, with the correct sound frequency, pitch and timing is almost an ordeal, which only fully trained and experienced persons can perform. That is why mere translation and recitation of a mantra in any language is not likely to produce the desired effect until the requisite frequency and pitch are also matched.

Besides the requirement of a specific pitch and frequency when chanting a mantra, the prescribed tune (laya) in terms of a specific pause in the verbal pronunciation of words is also very important. In verbal pronunciation, the pause between two words cannot be indicated by a comma as done in written text. The pause in verbal pronunciation has to be indicated by a short intermittent stop/break of sound. If the pause in the verbal pronunciation or tune of any mantra is slightly misplaced, it may convey quite a misleading meaning and negate the power of the mantra. This is also true in written text as well. For example, the misplacement of a comma entirely changes the meaning of two written texts as shown here: "kill not, spare him" versus "kill, not spare him." Similarly, the proper placement of a pause is very important in verbal pronunciation in order to safeguard the real meaning. For example, by using the symbol of "…" for the pause, the above example can be shown as: "kill not … spare him" versus "kill … not spare him." Thus, the entire meaning is changed by misplacing the pause. Mantras are generally written in a poetic verse form for brevity and easy remembrance. Hence, the prescribed tune with proper placement of pauses is very important for every mantra. This greatly affects the success of any mantra. In the Vedic period, all scriptures of the Vedas were composed in verse (hymn) form and remembered and sung as shruti knowledge. So, any mistake in tune and pauses in their singing is likely to misconstrue the real meaning and purpose of these verses. This is where many readers have committed mistakes and developed misconstructions of Vedic knowledge, bringing a bad reputation to the Vedas, especially around the period of 500 BCE and thereafter.

MANTRA SHAKTI has now become a great source of orthodoxy. In modern times, the power of mantra is being misused by some fraudulent priests and saints. These fraudulent priests and saints prescribe some mantra simply in terms of the words of the hymn without prescribing their manner of chanting in the specified raga or pitch, sound frequency, tune and pause, that too for achieving some objective far beyond the power of that mantra. For example, they may prescribe a mantra for worship of GANESHA to achieve more wealth. If wealth can be achieved just by chanting a mantra, who on earth would bother about tedious hard work, financial planning and management? On this, they may console the believer by saying that chanting the mantra of GANESHA for obtaining wealth may provide hope and help in concentrating on the methods of obtaining wealth. They say this only to counter the doubtful mind of a gullible believer. In fact, worshiping and praying to ISHWARA or some deity as a source of faith and trust gives solace, peace and hope to an anxious and worrying mind along with developing a sense of confidence and power of pursuance of the objective. But to say that worshiping a mantra will provide a key to an individual in pursuit of any cherished objective is camouflaging the intent of befooling and cheating. Practiced in this way, it has become an example of an orthodox ritual, inviting criticism from scientists and other rationalists. People need to be advised to damn such fraudsters. They should also be cautioned that the use of any mantra without full knowledge of its raga or tune, pitch and sound frequency may bring adverse results.

As a matter of fact, simple prayer alone is more purposeful in seeking some benevolence rather than running after some mantra. Prayers not only provide solace, peace and hope, but also empower the person with more confidence, contentment and virtuousness. There are many prayers with different emphases on seeking empowerment, enlightenment or benevolence. One very simple and common prayer to achieve empowerment of the self is: "O GOD, grant me the serenity to accept the things that I cannot change, the courage to achieve what I can, and the wisdom to know the difference." This short prayer can be easily translated into any language, may help provide peace, strength and vision, and can be recited anytime anywhere without any worship paraphernalia. Another very common prayer is the GAYATRI Mantra, which is basically a prayer in a poetic form and is quite suitable for adoration and meditation. As a prayer, it can be recited by anyone but in the prescribed manner of pronunciation of words of the poem. It is a prayer to the Divine for granting knowledge, enlightenment and energy (GYAN, PRAKASH and URJA). In a poetic form, it can be easily obtained nowadays from the internet or any temple. These are only a few examples to convey to the general people that prayers serve a better purpose than mantras, which require very specific and arduous training before being practiced. Instead of going for the tough task of reciting mantras, prayers should be made to implore or invoke the deity to help in a crisis.

3.2.4 Significance of Aum

The word AUM, commonly pronounced as OM, has been variedly signified in ancient as well as modern religious literature in India. It is used as a precursor in all mantras and prayers, during any worship ceremony. It is also used as a pious symbol. Primarily, it is accorded three important characteristics of being SANATAN, SHASHVAT and KALYANKARI, i.e., it is eternal, omnipresent and benedictory. These three characteristics could be so proven if the meaning of AUM is scientifically understood and practiced. Scientifically speaking, the word AUM is a spectrum of three natural sounds that are produced when one opens the mouth full, makes a sound from the vocal cords, and then quickly closes the mouth while continuing to make the humming sound for a few seconds. In this process, without using the tongue, lips or other parts of the mouth cavity, the three natural sounds are produced in a sequence, which are those of the letter A, as in "AAH" when the mouth is full open, next of the letter U, as in "OOH" when the mouth is being closed, and the next of letter "M", as in "MMH" giving the humming sound when the mouth is fully closed. These three sounds, pronounced together in sequence, make the combined sound of AUM. The combined sound of "A" and "U" generates the sound of "O", which together with the sound of "M" generates a sound like "OM". Thus, AUM is a spectrum of three natural sounds produced by the throat, using only vocal cords without any special maneuver of other sound-producing organs such as the tongue, lips, jaw and mouth cavity, and also without any specific thought and language.

Being natural sounds—without the use of the tongue, lips or jaw—these sounds occur in some way everywhere, all the time, since humans began speaking, through someone's or another's full open, half closed and fully closed mouths, thus, creating a low micro-pitch sound of AUM quite often, at times even remaining unheard. Hence, it is called eternal and omnipresent. In this sense, it represents ISHWARA, who is eternal and omnipresent. It is said that if one's mind is made still and thoughtless, one can listen to this sound of 'AUM' as very slow vibrations emanating and echoing within oneself as well as those emanating and echoing everywhere in the universe. So, it is also called as "ANHAD NAD", which means sound without the boundary of time and space. Thus, the word AUM does not belong to any specific language or regional setting or religion. The other words of any language in different regions and religions can be pronounced only when the sounds are produced through vocal cords by using the tongue, lips, jaws and mouth cavity in different ways and styles, according to phonetics and the pronunciation method of that particular language. But the sound of AUM is generated as a natural sound just through the vocal cords when a fully open mouth is quickly closed.

In fact, the first three basic alphabets that humans everywhere must have learned to express their primitive feelings were: "A" in pronouncing 'AAH' for pain when hurt, "U" in pronouncing 'OOH' for grief and sorrow, and "M" in pronouncing 'MMH' for relief and solace. Thus, these three alphabets made up the first language learned by the early human foragers. These three alphabets pronounced together in quick sequence make the word 'AUM' sound like 'OM'. Therefore, the sound 'AUM' or 'OM' is considered as SHANATAN and SHASHVAT as being the first syllable of human speech and is still continuing. Much later, when fully spoken languages were developed and theological thoughts and religion were also evolved, these three alphabets got the recognition of being the primordial sounds of "OMKAR" emanating from the super consciousness or cosmic energy. Therefore, 'OM' was also accorded the reverence of being ISHWARA itself. Thus, the word AUM has been signified variedly in the religious scriptures and is being used in several contexts. Nowadays, it has been made a cure for all woes by several priests.

To understand its KALYANKARI characteristic, one should learn the manner of chanting the word AUM. Chanting of this word is to be done for 10 to 15 minutes or more, in a scientific manner as explained earlier, i.e., open full mouth to make the sound and quickly close the mouth while making the sound. This makes one's mind completely still and thoughtless, which in itself is a cure for many woes. Often too much crowding of thoughts, troublesome problems and situations make the mind tense with mental, emotional or nervous strain. As a result, several psychosomatic (psychological and cellular) problems develop like muscular spasms, gastric disorders, circulatory disruptions in air or blood or the lymph system, pain in different parts of the body, etc. Normally, in a healthy body, the nerve cells of the mind called neurons send signals to the auto-immune system of the body for the cure/resolution of such psychosomatic disorders. But in a tense and strained mind, these neurons become entangled due to which nerve signals get disrupted, causing further nervous strain. When the mind becomes still and completely thoughtless after chanting AUM for some time, the neurons start becoming disentangled and gradually begin normal functions by sending nerve signals. As a result, the nervous strain and tension gradually reduce and the body starts feeling cured, relieved and relaxed. Therefore, the sound 'AUM' or 'OM' is considered as KALYANKARI. If the state of thoughtlessness is practiced and deep meditation is done regularly, the state of bliss can be achieved as the body will remain free of mental stress and the many associated health problems.

But chanting AUM in a rhythmic sequence through a fully open, half open and fully closed mouth, for 10 to 15 minutes daily as explained earlier, may be quite cumbersome to most people. So, an easy way to propagate is to chant AUM as one sound, i.e., OM, slowly in a somewhat melodious rhythm with the mind concentrating only on this chanting for some time. This shortcut is quite in practice nowadays during the beginning and/or end of prayers and yoga sessions. What matters is a distraction from the ambiance and concentration of the mind, which brings thoughtlessness together with a melodious sound frequency that soothes the tense mind and brings relief. The chanting of AUM or OM can be practiced any time anywhere but in a rather secluded and peaceful place so that concentration and serenity of the mind could be achieved. Also, to make it more effective, chanting must be done in a rhythmic manner in some melodious tune and possibly on an empty stomach so that it could be synchronized with deep breathing as well. This exercise is the most simple and effective way for achieving a stress-free mind and good health. This characteristic has accorded it great appeal and acceptance as being KALYANKARI.

It was the ancient rishis of India who discovered the significance of the word AUM, commonly pronounced as OM. They enunciated its importance in their Vedic religious and YOGIC literature as: it represents ISHWARA, it is NADA, a universal sound that is heard when the ears are closed, it is a BEEJ MANTRA giving rise to other mantras, and it is SANATAN, SHASVAT and KALYANKARI. They explained that chanting this mantra leads to four stages of an awakening of the consciousness: 'AA' connotes outward awakening in physical terms from the surrounding ambiance; 'UU' connotes inner awakening in feelings, thoughts, dreams and imaginations; 'MM' connotes deep inner awakening with complete thoughtlessness, finally leading to deep meditation. They prescribed chanting of this mantra of 'OM' exclusively during meditation. They also prescribed prefixing it to all other mantras and prayers during any religious ceremony with a connotation that it would enhance the power of other mantras and religious ceremonies. With the acceptance of its divine power, it has now become a standard practice to invocate help or support from ISHWARA by chanting OM at the beginning of any prayer or mantra.

3.2.5 Surya Namaskar and Arhgya

The beauty of the body is supported by the skeleton of bones and cartilage, which are dense calcified tissues. Modern medical science and nutrition studies suggest that with aging and also under some pathological conditions, the structure of bones and cartilage deteriorates and gets damaged, leading to serious problems of osteoporosis and/or osteoarthritis, affecting body movement. It is, therefore, essential to protect the structure of the bones and cartilage in terms of good mass density and strength. For this, calcium availability in sufficient quantities in the body is required through healthy food intake. The utilization of calcium in the body is made effective by vitamin D, without which the calcium remains unutilized and passes out as waste. Therefore, to ensure adequate utilization of calcium in the body, modern doctors recommend body exposure to the early morning sun for about 15 to 20 minutes, which produces the required amount of vitamin D in the body, or taking an oral supplement of vitamin D. The early morning sunshine is mild on the body and, hence, recommended. After about two hours of sunrise, the sunshine becomes quite harsh and pierces the body, causing sunburn and other associated skin ailments. This is modern medical advice to keep one fit and fine for regular and carefree movements.

The ancient rishis of India, especially Maharshi Patanjali, had discovered the benefit of the early morning sun in keeping the bones healthy. Though not exactly in terms of its providence for vitamin D, which as such was not discovered by then, they had visualized the benefic aspect of the early morning sun in keeping the body's bones healthy. To obtain this benefit from sunlight, they devised a ritual of offering water to the sun and called this offering ARGHYA to the Sun. They also devised the exercise of SURYA NAMASKAR as reverence to the Sun deity. Both these should be done in front of the early morning sun. Reverence to all the major elements of nature, like the sun, moon, earth, air, water, fire, etc., was the basic philosophy underlying the Vedic Sanatan religion to ensure they were preserved and avoid their degeneration by irrational exploitation by greedy people. This was intended to keep nature functional for the larger benefit of humanity. The exercise of SURYA NAMASKAR, as the name itself indicates, includes a set of 12 mini-exercises that should be performed in a sequence in front of the early morning sun. It would take about 15 to 20 minutes to complete the whole set of exercises.

The set of 12 exercises for SURYA NAMASKAR are so devised as to ensure the required movement of all the body parts to make them supple, functional and active. Thus, it would not only ensure the availability of vitamin D in the body through early morning exposure to the sun, but also make the bones and muscles supple and ready for the daily routine. Thus, the whole body would be recharged and energized in addition to full protection of the body's bone mass. But, as the name itself suggests, it should be performed in front of the early morning sun to get both benefits. If it is not performed in the open, in front of an early morning sun but performed at any other time and place, then it would simply become an exercise just to recharge muscles and energize the body. In that case, the benefit of ensuring the production of vitamin D in the body to keep the bones healthy will not be obtained. Then, after a certain age, oral supplements of vitamin D would be needed for those who do not work or move out enough in the open sunshine, especially urban dwellers in multistoried buildings and office workers. In fact, the benefits of exposing the body to the early morning sun are much more than those mentioned above. The early morning air is very fresh and free from pollution, the whole atmosphere is very calm and quiet, and birds are flying with pleasant and melodious chirping sounds. Being with nature in the early morning for a while generates a very serene and happy feeling in the heart and mind. Then even simple exercises like stretching, walking, moving, sitting, etc., help the release of happy hormones of serotonin and dopamine in the body, which make one feel better.

For some people, especially women folk and aged people, who for some reason cannot perform the set of 12 exercises, a way out for exposure to the rising sun was also developed and prescribed in the form of sun worship by an act of offering water to the early morning sun through a small jar of about one-liter capacity while chanting the sun worshiping mantra (hymn). This act is called offering ARGHYA to the SUN deity and is made a concluding part of the entire early morning worship. The water is poured slowly on the ground before the rising sun and the worship mantra is chanted repeatedly as many times as possible in about 10 to 15 minutes. The ancient rishis knew that ARGHYA water would not cool the sun or lower its intensity. The sun was and is still worshiped as a deity for heat energy and sunshine as the benevolence for food production and some medical care. So, they did not intend to cool the sun with ARGHYA water. In fact, they thought of this ritual as a way to bring women folk and aged persons out into the early morning sun. Thus, the ARGHYA ritual will sufficiently expose their body to the early morning sun for the assimilation of vitamin D in the body.

However, over time, the scientific reason and wisdom underlying this act got lost, and it has now become just an orthodox ritual in the morning worship that is completed by quickly pouring water on the ground in the name of the sun any time anywhere, not necessarily before the rising sun. In this way, it has surely become an example of an orthodox ritual, inviting criticism from scientists and other rationalists. If it cannot be done before the early morning sun, it should better be avoided rather than doing it as an orthodox ritual. In modern times, because of the rising population, multistoried complexes have been built wherein a large number of people live in small flats that do not have enough open space. Hence, performing the SURYA NAMASKAR and ARGHYA is not possible for residents of flats. In such cases, arrangements must be made on the top of the building by the owners or the housing society by marking and preparing a clean place for performing both these acts in rotation for gents and ladies. It will then become a cause for social gathering and cohesion, leading to a better social environment in addition to better health.

3.2.6 Kundalini Jagaran

In yogic literature, the term KUNDALINI JAGARAN refers to an activation of power chakras in the body, which constitute a complex energy system conceptualized in the ancient Vedas. There are seven main power chakras conceptualized as energy centers that are located along the spinal cord in the human body. The lowest chakra is called MULADHARA, located near the pelvic base of the spine. It deals with a sense of security and stability. The next chakra called SVADHISTHANA is located below the belly and deals with sexual and creative energy, and relates to emotions. The third chakra called MANIPURA is located along the stomach area and is responsible for confidence and self-esteem. The fourth chakra called ANAHATA is located near the heart, in the center of the chest, and deals with compassion and the ability to love. The fifth chakra called VISHUDDHA is located near the throat and deals with the ability of verbal communication. The sixth chakra called AJNA is located between the two eyes and is linked to intuition and imagination, also known as the third eye. The seventh chakra called

SAHASTRARA is located at the top of the head and spine and is the crown chakra, representing the spiritual level. These chakras are conceptualized as the invisible subtle forces, not as any physical part of the body. These invisible forces of the chakras regulate the energy system of our body. When these chakras are active, the body is healthy and fully energetic. But when these chakras become passive, the body becomes sick and dull.

These chakras have some similarities with the endocrine glands system of the body discovered in modern medical science. The set of five endocrine glands, which secrete several hormones to properly regulate major body functions, seem to have some correspondence with the six body chakras mentioned above and are located above the MULADHARA chakra. The sex glands of the testes and ovaries are located below the belly, which respectively secrete testosterone and estrogen to regulate the male and female characteristics and have a corresponding similarity with the SVADHISTHANA chakra. The adrenal glands and pancreas are located along the stomach and respectively secrete adrenaline and insulin to regulate stress response, blood pressure and blood sugar, having a corresponding similarity with the MANIPURA chakra. The thymus gland is located along the heart region, behind the breastbone, and is responsible for producing and maturing lymphocytes or the immune system and has a corresponding similarity with the ANAHATA chakra. The thyroid glands are located near the throat and secrete triiodothyronine, thyroxin, calcitonin and parathyroid to regulate metabolism, bone health, and calcium absorption through vitamin D in the body, and have a corresponding similarity with VISUDDHA chakra. The pineal gland is located deep in the brain and secretes the melatonin hormone, which regulates sleep and alertness and has a corresponding similarity with the AJNA chakra. Pituitary and hypothalamus glands are located inside the head, at the top of the spine, and secrete several hormones that stimulate other hormonal systems to influence the nervous system, reproduction and growth in the body, and have a corresponding similarity with the SAHASTRARA chakra. Thus, correspondence between the chakras and endocrine glands does have some resemblance indicative of scientific wisdom underlying these chakras visualized as invisible forces by ancient rishis.

The body chakras can be activated by a set of activities that include: (1) yoga asana, (2) pranayama, and (3) deep meditation and Samadhi, thereby KUNDALINI JAGARAN can be achieved. Some ancient rishis used to practice this for going into deep meditation and Samadhi by activating all chakras and finally reaching activated SAHATRARA, the crown chakra, to enter Samadhi and enjoy the state of BLISS of consciousness in the cosmos garden. In this state, they could and did travel across the solar system and galaxy in a subtle form. This is part of the famous Indian MYSTIC. This is how they described several planets in the Vedas, and some of those descriptions are found to be quite similar to those now brought out by the recent space investigations. But, the tedious processes for activation of the centers of power chakras and KUNDALINI JAGRAN are not only difficult ordeals, even for saints and rishis, but are also quite dangerous until followed under the supervision of a highly accomplished yogi. These processes would not be easily comprehensible to the common people and, therefore, should not be attempted by them. However, an easily comprehensible and practicable simple version of KUNDALINI JAGARAN for the common people is thought of and suggested as follows for all those desiring to practice it.

For the common people, the most practicable version of KUNDALINI JAGARAN is suggested here as simply an activation of the functions of the stomach and intestines in the body, which anybody can practice if so desired. The term KUNDALINI refers to the coiled intestinal structure, both small and large intestines, which is located along the region between the naval and groin, i.e., just above the pelvic region and are placed as circular rounded coiled structures (like KUNDALI of a siting snake). The ingested food material is thoroughly mixed with digestive acids and juices in the stomach, and thereafter, it is passed on to the intestines for assimilation and absorption in the body. So, in common parlance, KUNDALINI JAGARAN may also refer simply to the activation of the stomach and intestines. The intestines thoroughly digest and absorb all food that is received from the stomach. The intestines absorb the nutrients of vitamins, minerals and glucose required for the blood and body cells and send the leftover waste to the anus for excretion. Thus, they provide an energy source for the whole body. Therefore, proper activation of the stomach and intestines is crucial for good health and can be called KUNDALINI JAGARAN in common parlance or layman's terms. In other words, it means activating MANIPURA chakra in yogic terms. In terms of modern medical science, it means activating the adrenal glands and pancreas, thereby regulating blood pressure, blood sugar and stress response.

In ancient times, after practicing full KUNDALINI JAGARAN through activation of all the chakras, the ascetic saints and rishis, called yogis, used to eat a bare minimum of food, only once a day and spent several days in meditation and Samadhi. In meditation and Samadhi, though energy requirements get greatly reduced, some energy is needed for cell regeneration and cutaneous respiration. Energy from the initial food intake gets stored in blood cells as glucose and in the liver as a capacitor in the form of fat for gradual release at a later period, whenever needed. There are some austere living people who eat normal food only once a day and work all day without any fatigue. Their KUNDALINI is more active. On the other hand, many affluent people eat food four or more times a day and still feel lethargic and tired because of weak KUNDALINI. What matters is the capacity to utilize food through better digestive power, which means activating the KUNDALINI of the intestines. Then a small quantum of food intake will be sufficient to maintain all body functions.

For hard manual work about 2400 calories, for light work about 1800 calories, and for no extra work but only daily routine activities about 1000 calories of energy are required. This serves as the broad guideline for the quantity of food intake for different types of people. Among all the large animals, only pigs convert about 25-30 percent of their food intake into body mass. In humans, normally 15-20 percent of the total food intake is digested and converted into the above-said nutrients and body mass to enable the body to carry out activities. The rest is passed out as waste and excreted. Further, an overfilled stomach or overeating reduces digestive power, and hence, the utilization of food in that case is even lesser and most of it is wasted and excreted. Therefore, to increase the utilization of food, activation of KUNDALINI, i.e., increasing the digestive power of the stomach and intestines, is required. This is the crux of simple KUNDALINI JAGRAN for the common people.

The full KUNDALINI JAGRAN can be done by practicing yoga and pranayama along with the prescribed rituals of YAM and NIYAM to be followed, and the gradual reduction of food intake over a long period of time. However, this will be an ordeal requiring great endurance and forbearance along with the guidance of an accomplished teacher. This will be beyond the forbearance of the common people. For the common people, simply practicing some relevant asanas and pranayama along with the gradual reduction of food intake as per the calorie requirement, as stated above, will help activate the digestive power and KUNDALINI of the intestines. This will greatly reduce the body's dependence on a large quantum of food intake for nutrients and energy requirements as the intestines will be activated to convert more amount of food intake into more nutrients and energy, which will reduce the amount of food waste for excretion. Then, not only will the overall food requirements at the individual, country and world levels be greatly reduced, but external energy requirements for the production and processing of large amounts of food will also be drastically reduced. This is the great message of yoga to the world, besides the simple fitness message.

3.2.7 Marriage Ceremony

In the Vedic Sanatan religion, marriage is solemnized as a socio-religious ceremony and not as a contract. Making it a socio-religious ceremony means involving ISHWARA and other deities in some of its rituals, which makes the marriage sacrosanct. This makes the marriage more stable, i.e., it cannot be easily annulled, as people generally abide by religious rites. In the Vedic Sanatan tradition of marriage, first match-making is done based on the horoscopes of both, the boy and girl. The horoscopes prepared from their birth charts make astrological predictions about certain humane qualities of both and their suitability in the proposed marriage bond is checked. Many people question the validity of this match-making done based on a birth chart or horoscope that is prepared using astrology. These people advocate a different system for match-making through dating between a boy and girl for better knowing and understanding each other. But they perhaps do not know that the divorce rates are much higher in marriages based on match-making through dating. Dating is very common in western and some other countries, where divorce rates are also very high as a marriage is generally considered a contract that can be easily annulled by a decree of the court. Therefore, in match-making through dating, there is no security and guarantee for a happy and joint living forever because dating usually leads to infatuation or fondness and rarely to love and understanding for each other.

The debate on the alternative match-making procedure involves the moot question of granting individual liberty to youngsters to choose their own life partners for marriage and then face the likely consequence themselves versus asking them to accept the marriage settled by their family and face the likely consequence together with the family. There are several issues involved in the case of individual liberty used in the selection of a life partner without the involvement of the family. First, in case of separation, the high time lag generally involved in the settlement of a divorce case in the court of law and the legal arrangements for care and guardianship of the children during and after the settlement of the court case need be considered. These matters are not as easy as the dating procedure; emotions and the future of the children are involved therein. Second, individual liberty should have an interface with the value system adopted by the family and society. The absence of this interface gives rise to a lot of socio-economic as well as legal problems, such as maternity and infant care, the occasional need for psycho-therapeutic care, disposal of family assets, etc. Western countries have evolved this interface through a change in their social values and its general acceptance. They have evolved an alternate system for the emerging socio-economic and legal problems, such as only hospitalized maternity care, babysitting culture, psychiatric consultancy and clinics, disowning family lineage, etc., and are now bearing out its good or bad consequences. In the absence of such an interface, individual liberty and social values always clash with each other, leading to family feuds and social conflicts.

In the Vedic Sanatan religion, a family-settled and religiously performed marriage is more common. Such a marriage has a far lesser chance of divorce due to the built-in process of mutual adjustment through religious and social pressures. In this case, other problems either do not emerge or are taken care of jointly in the family. In modern times, however, a compromised method of combining both the individual's choice as well as a family-settled relationship has evolved, which is a good and better way of maintaining tradition with modernity. In this method, after pre-final talks on the marriage proposal, including horoscope matching, a meeting of the boy and girl is arranged at some suitable place for their mutual talk and agreement. When both, the boy and girl, give their consent for each other, an auspicious date is chosen, after consulting a priest, for conducting the actual marriage ceremony. In the Vedic tradition, all religious ceremonies are performed on auspicious dates suggested by priests as per the astrological calendar in order to minimize unexpected adversaries while conducting the ceremony or thereafter. The marriage ceremony involves some dowry payment (notional or actual) as a parting gift from the father to the daughter, a feast for all participants, worship of ISHWARA and some deities for blessing, the conduct of seven PHERES, i.e., seven circular rounds of a mutual oath taken by the bride and bridegroom before the pious fire while being joined together through a circular knot in their scarves. It is believed that this circular knot and oath before the pious fire keep both tied together for their whole lives.

Originally, the concept of dowry was to give the marrying daughter's share in the father's property to the bridegroom's father so that the daughter-in-law is not considered a liability on them. But later, it became a greedy negotiated deal and a curse that has labeled daughters as an undesirable burden on parents. Earlier, marriage was like forming a cooperative team between two families in which money, pomp and show were not important. Hence, dowry was simply a willing and parting gift called as "NEG and KANYADAN" by the father. Later, marriage became like a corporate affair in which money and status through dowry became an important consideration and, hence, dowry became a greedy negotiated deal. Nowadays, a new trend is emerging, which is making marriage like a king's and queen's coronation, in which, besides dowry, great pomp and show using all modern technologies is becoming more of a fashion trend like those weddings shown in cinema and TV shows. These trends are tremendously increasing the expenditures incurred in performing marriages and are obviously borne by the bride's parents. To many not-so-well-off parents, this new trend is now becoming a curse. Also, such ostentatious shows just for a day/night represent more of a waste of resources rather than a glamor and prestige show-off.

The feast for the participants is given in two parts, first at the bridegroom's place in a pre-marriage ceremony to commemorate the settlement of marriage, and second at the bride's place to complete the marriage ceremony. The purpose of the feast is to invite relatives, friends and other known people to witness the marriage ceremony and accept the bride and bridegroom as a married couple. Worship of ISHWARA and deities for blessings is to make the marriage sacrosanct. The conduct of the seven PHERES, i.e., seven circular rounds of mutual oath-taking before the pious fire, is performed to administer a moral pledge by both the bride and bridegroom about the seven commandments of virtuous and happy living. This conduct of seven PHERES is done in the presence of senior members of both families and is solemnized by the priest through the Vedic mantras spoken in the Sanskrit language. Thus, this special ceremony imposes a moral binding on both the bride and bridegroom to care, share and be responsible for each other. Gifts by relatives and acquaintances are primarily a social ritual. Finally, the marriage ceremony is concluded with a farewell function.

3.2.8 Multitude of Festivals

Festivity brings joy and happiness, makes people especially active and breaks the monotony in life. In the Vedic Sanatan religion, some festivals are celebrated as worship of an avatar of ISHWARA or some deity, some festivals relate to the weather and some to periodic transitions of the moon and sun. Because of a multitude of avatars and deities, there are many festivals on this account itself. Then there are weather seasons and agricultural harvest seasons that are also celebrated with full joy and festivity. Some festivities relate to the worship of the moon and sun as the natural sources of coolness and heat energy in the environment. Worship of different positions of the moon, e.g., full moon (called PURNIMA), no moon (called AMAVASHYA) and the eleventh moon (called EKADASHI) are being regularly done religiously. The world-famous Deepawali festival is celebrated on a no moon day of AMAVASHYA before the start of winter. Likewise, worship of the sun is done quite religiously with great enthusiasm as Chattha Puja, about six days after the Deepawali festival. Similarly, the great social unity festival of Holi is celebrated on a full moon day of PURNIMA after winter. Thus, there is a multitude of festivals. Almost every month, one or two festivals are celebrated making life quite dynamic, vibrant and non-monotonous.

However, these festivals were conceived and celebrated not simply as religious ceremonies or for joy and pastime. In addition to religion, joy and merriment, these festivals also have some better and more scientific reasons and logic for celebrations. The first scientific reason is that some sort of fasting, usually half-day fasting, is associated with many festivals. But in a few festivals, even full-day fasting is done. The ancient science of health in Ayurveda recognized the benefits of periodic fasting in keeping the body and mind fit. Modern medical science also advises regular intermittent fasting and some occasional periodic fasting in the body fitness routine. So, the multitude of festivals serve to provide for periodic fasting for better health and fitness. The second scientific reason is that special food is generally prepared in some festivals using some uncommon food items that do not form part of the food basket in daily meals. This helps break the food monotony. This also supplements the body requirement of some specific micro-nutrients, which are available only in those uncommon food items. These uncommon food items cannot form part of the regular daily meal for some or other reason, such as only specialized seasonal production in small measure and/or seasonal requirement in small quantity or some peculiar taste, etc. So, these uncommon foods are included in the food basket only on some specific festivity. Further, the regular seasonal agricultural harvest brings new types of food grains, vegetables, fruits and spices that are used in some seasonal festive foods. This brings a seasonal change in the diet pattern, meets the multi-food requirement in the food basket and also fulfills the periodic fasting requirement for better health and mood wellness.

The third socially logical reason is that some festivals are celebrated for family reunions, especially the festival of Deepawali, which is celebrated before winter and the festival of Holi, celebrated after the winter season. Both these festivals are celebrated with great enthusiasm, especially by the children who are more eager for the joy of festivity. The out-stationed members return home to celebrate these festivals, and join the whole family in the worship, feast and joy celebrations, which run over a few days. This family get-together strengthens the family bond and provides a sense of oneness and security among the elder members of the family. In particular, the Holi festival is celebrated for the larger union and get-together in which relatives, friends and cohabitants of an area all meet each other and exchange greetings and well wishes. This helps in building a cohesive and compassionate society. In addition, these family union type festivities provide a forum for the cultural orientation of the younger generation, which usually lives far away from the senior family members, generally in a different social setup. Thus, all the festivals have some sound scientific and/or social logic, wisdom and philosophy.

In ancient times and till a few decades earlier, these festivals were celebrated in a simple way but with great zeal and enthusiasm, and did not cause any disturbance or nuisance to those not celebrating. But recently, some festivals, especially Deepawali and Holi, have been overloaded with modern technological gimmicks to make it more of a pomp and show. This is causing not only disturbance and nuisance to those not celebrating, but also causing harmful pollution to the environment such as air and noise pollution by high decibel crackers and light pollution by glittering and sparkling lights used in decorations during the Deepawali festival, and varied types of adhesive chemical colors causing skin and breathing allergies during the Holi festival. There is no logic and wisdom involved in the ostentatious pomp and show or nuisance activities. Neither modern science and rationality nor ancient science of logic and wisdom support the outrageous ostentation and nuisance that causes unnecessary trouble and harm to others through one's festivity. Such acts by some blockheaded persons simply make a mockery of some rituals associated with these grand festivals, and this must be severely resented and banned. Otherwise, others are bound to call the festival an orthodox show. The sentiments and emotions of others not celebrating a particular festival must be duly respected, otherwise, cohesiveness in the society gets lost, leading to unnecessary fractions and group animosity.

3.2.9 Respect for Elders

The word elder connotes seniority in age with which normally more experience of life is associated. Hence, it is customary to pay respect to the elderly in most societies around the world. However, the manner of paying respect varies in different societies. In some societies, youngsters simply address the elders in the family with the words 'Hi' or 'Hello' in the same way as they do to their peers and others. This manner does not express any special feeling towards the elders who often feel a sense of neglect for being treated just like others. In some other societies, youngsters bow before the elders in the family to convey their respect to them. In some societies, youngsters use some respectable words while addressing the elderly in the family to convey their respect to them. In both these latter cases, the elders are accorded some special respect as compared to other members of the family. In India, among those who follow the Vedic Sanatan religion, there is a tradition of youngsters touching the feet not only of the elderly in the family but also of many other respectable persons like teachers, accomplished saints, highly learned persons, etc. There is quite a curiosity in some other societies about this tradition of touching the feet of the elderly in the family and some other respectable persons. Some even consider this tradition a simply backward orthodox ritual.

There is a Shakespearean saying that nothing is good or bad but thinking makes it so. Therefore, a particular choice is simply a matter of preference over the other. However, at all such places and in all such groups where decorum and discipline are regarded as highly desirable, e.g., in a classroom or in the military, certain protocol is prescribed for meeting and addressing, especially senior persons. In a similar manner, the Vedic Sanatan religion prescribes touching elders' feet and those of other respectable persons as a protocol for maintaining decorum and discipline, which is necessary for keeping peace, harmony and belongingness in the family and society. By touching the feet of an elder, the youngster conveys to the elder that I am still at the ground level, near your feet, and you are above me at your height with all your experience and achievements. This is a respectful acknowledgment to the elder that your experience and achievements in life are above all my worth, which, in fact, has been possible due to your sacrifices for me. This is not simply an expression of gratitude, but also an expression of love with reverence. This develops a feeling of belongingness in the family and helps the youngster shun the ego of superiority on account of his own recent achievements.

It is quite visible in those societies not having any special formal way of acknowledging respect for the elders that youngsters often take undue liberty in doing whatever they feel like doing without caring for the sentiments, emotions and advice of the elders. Youngsters do not pay heed at all to the elders, much less listen to their advice. This often creates a feeling of neglect and alienation among the elders in the family. Over time, this often serves as a major cause of disintegration of the family. This is the main reason why and how the institution of family is eroding in such societies. It is not the generation gap that is often blamed for this family disquiet and disintegration, but it is the lack of respect for elders who have made sacrifices for the well-being and growth of the youngsters. The absence of proper respect for elders and decorum in the family makes youngsters develop some sort of feeling of being smarter and modern, which often clashes with the opinions of some senior members of the family. This type of snob-attitude and the resultant clashes are also seen, even among the youngsters themselves, in schools, playgrounds, roads, offices, etc., as is being witnessed more these days. Therefore, some more conspicuous form of decorum is needed in addressing seniors in the family, which could teach youngsters to shun snobbery.

It is not a question of withdrawing the liberty of children or youngsters in their own game of life. But the issue of enforcing decorum and discipline among all living together needs to be properly addressed, or else some sort of separatism and alienation is obvious. Politeness, courtesy and mutual care are the bonding glues for all types of togetherness. Touching the feet of the elders in the family and other respected persons in the society is just one way the ancient Vedic Sanatan religion thought of, which helped save the family from disintegration and contributed to a better social environment. There may be some other ways that the modern proponents of unrestricted liberty and rights may have to think of to save the institutions of family and society, which have so far served humanity in its growth and development over the millenniums so well. There should be some balance between individual liberty and social values, otherwise, the existence of great institutions of family, society and cooperation will be at a vulnerable risk as is now visible in many parts of the world. In the absence of family and society, individuals are likely to become human robots, running and fighting the rat race of technological development without humane feelings, emotions, compassion and cooperation.

3.2.10 Karma Aur Karmafal

BHAGVAT GITA is one of the most widely read and acclaimed ancient Indian religious scriptures, nationally as well as internationally. One of its most widely quoted dictum states, 'do your karma (action) which is your duty, do not bother about karmafal (result).' This is what Lord Krishna advised Arjuna on the battlefield of Kurukshetra in the great ancient epic of Mahabharata. But the desire to achieve success in one's endeavor is quite inevitable because it is the expectation of some result that gives rise to the urge to do karma (action) in most cases. Without the expectation of any karmafal (result), most people would simply loiter or saunter away doing nothing. Then how would the world progress and exhibit its varied diversity? The world would then become just another piece of inert matter like many other planets. This is certainly not what Lord Krishna intended to convey to Arjuna on the battlefield. While drawing any inference, one should always keep in mind the reference and context of any saying. So, what Lord Krishna actually conveyed is that 'once in any battlefield of life, simply concentrate on doing your karma and not be drifted away with worries about the outcome.' The world has accepted and acclaimed this dictum of BHAGVAT GITA since ancient times.

Life is full of happenings. These happenings can be analyzed and appreciated by understanding the underlying forces operating in the three dimensions. The first dimension is that of the force of the genome, which describes the heritage of lineage in terms of active and dormant genes summarized in the DNA of an individual. The genome contains characteristic features of an individual in terms of personality and potential, which set out the contour of KARMA, i.e., the work that can be performed by an individual. Genome describes the intent and potential for different types of work in an individual and outlines what type of work can be performed easily and the extent of success possible in it, i.e., likely KARMAFAL or success. The second dimension is that of the force of upbringing or the environment in which an individual grows up. The environment includes a wide canvas from domestic fabric to educational, social and occupational build-ups all of which further shape the personality and create the capability of an individual over and above the force of the genome. The personality creates excitement, urge or provocation for certain types of work, and capability decides the approach and effort to be put into completing the work. Thus, if certain work is planned and performed according to the personality and capability, then success is more likely to flow in. The third dimension is that of the force of chance, which includes all those miscellaneous factors, benign and/or malign, beyond the control of an individual, but which un-intentionally occur and influence both the work and the success. The net KARMAFAL, i.e., result, is an outcome of the interaction of all the above forces in the three dimensions.

Scientists and other thinkers have attempted to study the above forces in more detail. Medical scientists and biotechnologists have studied DNA and deciphered the genome and the genetic code shaping the intent and potential, i.e., personality. However, they found it not advisable to alter the genetic configuration in human cells for ethical reasons. They have successfully done it through genetic engineering in some plants and animals. In the case of human beings, however, they have found the genetic information available through genome studies quite useful for medical and healthcare purposes. Psychologists and psychiatrists have studied various psycho-disorders affecting personality and capability in performing some desired works and developed some psychotherapy suiting individual cases. Similarly, sociologists, educationists and management experts have also developed a multitude of solutions for other environmental build-ups, affecting personality and capability in performing various types of work. For example, how to parent and guide children for careers suitable for them, how to make teaching interesting and ensure better and focused attendance in classrooms, how to solve peer group problems and motivate workers for better creativity and productivity, etc.

Some thinkers have also attempted to study and do an analysis of the chance factors affecting karma and karmafal. The statisticians simply call chance factors as errors in the forecast model due to the model being not fully specified, i.e., some important factor(s) left out. But, most of the time, it may be difficult to comprehend all the chance factors affecting any karma. The devout religious people call these chance factors as the will of GOD/ ISHWARA, which have to be accepted as they are. Some religious priests call these chance factors as the carryover effects of the previous birth karmas, which also have to be accepted as they are. The astrologers and palmists correlate these chance factors to the planetary constellations and may suggest some way out like wearing some gem or doing some worship but the outcome may be as uncertain as the chance factors themselves. The chance factors can be divided into two groups, one that is improbable and occurs at random, such as a sudden fire breakout affecting a karma, and a second that is probable and can be forecasted based on the probability of occurrence such as heavy rain affecting a karma. One can, at the most, take advantage of the probable factors by avoiding these if their forecast is available. Whether it is an error or the will of GOD/ISHWARA, carryover of a previous birth or the effect of a planetary constellation, by and large, it has to be taken for granted in accepting the karmafal or result.

Then, some people turn to priests for worship to please the ISHWARA or some deity, and some others turn to astrologers for help through gems and other possible techniques. The resorts to priests and astrologers are generally called as orthodox by the rationalists. The types of roadside priests and astrologers generally available and rendering help to most of the desirous people fall in the category of those called as orthodox. But astrology and gemology have been accepted for some problem diagnostics and treatments, if conducted by well-qualified and authentic practitioners. However, if the suggestion of some priest or astrologer provides some solace and peace to a perplexed mind, it may need to be verified whether it is just psychotherapy or really a resolution to the problem. Some people, such as accomplished saints, do possess extrasensory perception or a strong intuitive judgment and make suggestions that serve as a good resolution to the chance problem. But finding such a person may also be a matter of chance. So, the final result of karma may still remain a matter of chance unfolding in most cases. However, if some person is lucky enough to miss the role of chance factor altogether in his/her endeavor, it would provide a boost in saying that one is the maker of one's own destiny.

3.2.11 Astrology

It is said that the past is history, the future is a mystery, and the present is the best gift of nature and GOD/ISHWARA, so enjoy and live the present more happily. But the mystery of the future has always attracted the curiosity of the human mind. Indian astrology provides a way to look into this mystery as well as history. Astrology plays an important role in the religion. In the Vedic Sanatan religion, all the ceremonies, especially the new programs, are performed on an auspicious day to ensure their successful and hurdle-free completion. The concept of an auspicious day is a twin idea. One, there are some general auspicious days, which can be found in the religious calendar called a PANCHANG, which is prepared every year based on the current planetary constellation. For starting any ceremony or program, some general auspicious days for the purpose of the event can be found in the current PANCHANG and one day out of these can be selected for the start. Second, for any special ceremony or program for the specific individual, the specific auspicious days are worked out based on the individual's birth chart as well as the current PANCHANG and one of these is selected for the purpose. Thus, the role of astrology in determining the current planetary constellations for preparing the current PANCHANG and finding the general auspicious day or the specific auspicious day is very important in religion. However, like other religious ceremonies, astrology has also been criticized as being unscientific, illogical and orthodoxy by some scientists and rationalists. Yet since ages, it has remained an important socio-religious custom to consult an astrologer for an auspicious start of any new activity.

The science of astrology comprises two parts, one is the ancient science of astronomy known as JYOTIRVIGYANA, and the second is the art of prophesy through stargaze called as NAKSHATRA SHASHTRA. Thus, astrology is both science and art. The ancient astronomy deals with the study of movements of stars and planets, and employs a great deal of mathematics in the estimation of trajectory, periodicity and location of various planets in the solar constellation over time. Ancient astronomy is very scientific, swift and accurate in the calculation of the trajectory and distances of various stars and planets from earth, for which it uses only ancient Vedic mathematics that helps in rapid calculations of location, distance and their movements without the use of any calculator/computer. Periodic calculations of solar and lunar eclipses as also of occasional special alignments of certain stars and planets as made by ancient astronomy have been found to be perfectly matching with those made by modern astronomy. Thus, ancient astronomy is perfectly scientific. For making a prophecy, astrology makes use of the ancient nakshatra shastra. After studying the size, nature and trajectory of various stars and planets, ancient astrologers developed a complete treatise on stargaze called nakshatra shastra, which presents the good and bad influences of every individual star and planet as also of its interactions with other stars and planets. The veracity of these good and bad influences was regularly tested and vouched for over time through actual case studies of ancient predictions. Thus, the interpretations of stargazing or nakshatra shastra are not scientific and involve only skill and art.

Using ancient astronomy, the exact location, period of stay in that location, distance from the earth and relative movements of various stars and planets in the constellation of the solar system at the time of birth of an individual is used to prepare a birth chart. The birth chart shows the positions of various stars and planets and their interactions with each other at the time of the individual's birth. Using this birth chart and the nakshatra shastra, first the veracity of both is tested through some predictions of the past and then prophesies are made about the future curiosities of the individual. Ancient astronomy is considered quite scientific as its calculations match perfectly with those of modern astronomy. It is nakshatra shastra whose veracity is doubted to be unscientific by scientists and rationalists. They question how any far-off planet can cause good or bad effects on any individual. So, they call astrological predictions as orthodox. There are many renowned astrologists and many renowned astrological forums in the country that strongly believe in and are engaged in astrological predictions, propagation and publication of various magazines and books on the subject. But, by and large, they seem to have not attempted an explanation of the scientific rationality underlying the nakshatra shastra in terms of the known modern science to clear the orthodoxy charge.

The genetic mutations caused by cosmic rays at the time of birth do offer some explanation regarding the influence of stars and planets on human life. At the time of birth, the fetus comes out of the womb as an infant and faces the outside atmosphere for the first time. Inside the womb, it was fully protected from any external impact. But at the time of birth, the infant is most vulnerable to external impacts while facing the outside atmosphere for the first time. It is then that the cosmic rays pervading all around may cause some genetic mutation in the somatic cells. Indian mythology emanating from religion states that the living body is made up of five elements of nature, viz. air, water, earth, fire and sky. Whereas most people easily understand the role of four elements—air, water, earth and fire—they mostly fail to understand the role of the sky in shaping a living body. The sky puts its element in the living body through cosmic rays at the time of birth, which may cause genetic mutation and may lead to the exhibition of some special characteristics in the child as an effect of the cosmic rays from stars and planetary constellations at the time of birth. Thus, planetary constellations, especially at the time of birth, do affect an individual's body and mind. Such genetic mutations, due to cosmic rays, may also occur in the later periods of life depending upon the susceptibility of an individual to such radiations as a special case. But it cannot be generalized as a possibility.

The sun is about 150 million kilometers away from the earth. The light, heat and ultraviolet rays from the sun from such a far-off distance affect all the life on earth, including humans, animals, plants, trees and micro-organisms. The intensity of these radiations from the sun varies with time, according to changes in day and night as also due to changes in the seasons on earth; therefore, their effect on the somatic cells of living beings also varies with time. All the planets of the solar system move around the sun in their respective elliptical orbits, at times being closer to the sun, and at other times, being a little far off. These planets reflect the radiations received from the sun admixed with their own radiations to earth. Thus, cosmic radiations from these planets on earth also vary according to their being closer or farther from the sun, being day or night and the changing seasons on earth. In addition, there may also be radiations received on earth from other stars of the galaxy. All these radiations, received directly from the sun or via other planets and from other stars, constitute what are called as cosmic rays/radiations on earth. These cosmic rays/radiations may cause somatic mutations in the genetic structure of the newly born infant at the time of birth for being very vulnerable in facing the external environment for the first time. These somatic mutations, when occur, can influence the personality and potential components of an individual and, thereby one's thoughts, actions and achievements in life. That is why the exact details of time and place of birth are sought for making a birth chart because these details determine the intensity of the various types of cosmic radiations, thereby the influence of specific stars and planets in the birth chart. Thus, the accuracy of astrological predictions primarily depends upon the accuracy of the birth chart, which, in turn, depends on the correct birth time and place details. The astrological constellation as per the astronomy chart may vary in different places and in different time periods within a gap of about half an hour.

The experiments done in agricultural sciences on short-term exposure of plant seeds to extremely mild nuclear radiations have shown promising results in terms of somatic (cellular) mutations, causing changes in some plant characteristics such as dwarf plant size, resistance to some diseases, fruiting patterns, etc. Therefore, the above-said scientific explanation for cosmic rays from stars and planets affecting the life of any individual in terms of his/her potential and personality is quite understandable. But, as such, it does not explain that cosmic rays from any star or planet can bring any jackpot gain or sudden loss or some catastrophe to an individual. But astrologers looking through the birth chart of an individual often make such predictions about some good or bad event due to the benignant or malignant position of some star or planet in the birth chart, and then suggest some remedial measures like wearing a specific gem or doing some specific worship. On the face of it, this looks like a case of some fraudster doing an orthodox practice. However, the case of the influence of a gem in this regard is also somewhat understandable as the gem may modify some cosmic radiations, even during the later periods of the life of some vulnerable individual, depending upon the structure and shape of the gem that determines its strength and carat value. The significance of mantras and worship in this regard has already been explained earlier in section 3.2.3 of this chapter.

In fact, astrology is both science and art as already explained above in the beginning itself. As a matter of fact, every science has an associated component of art in it, which is called the intuitive skill of understanding and doing science. This intuitive skill is quite different from the professional skill of handling and managing scientific instruments and experiments. It is seen that all doctors and engineers selected through the same admission test are provided the same training by the same teachers in the same institution but do not perform in the exact identical way/manner in their profession due to differences in the intuitive skills acquired during their training. In the case of astrologers, it also applies in the same way. Many of these astrologers learn the scientific calculations of Vedic astronomy for preparing and reading a birth chart but fail to develop an intuitive skill for interpreting nakshatra shastra, which is not even scientific. Therefore, their astrological practice done mechanically does not do justice to the profession and brings a bad name to astrology. In fact, astrology and astrologers are two different entities, and both should not be mixed together; the former is a discipline and the latter is a disciple. But there are many astrologers who do full justice to the profession and have earned good names and fame as astrologers. Their success gives credence and recognition to astrology as a science and art.

But this brings to focus the basic question of how to explain the benevolent or malignant characteristics of different stars and planets. Science treats these stars and planets simply as matter condensed in different forms in the universe after the BIG BANG, and matter as such is inert and does not possess such influences of being benevolent or malignant. However, it is possible to differentiate the radiations from each star and planet individually as well as in interaction with other stars and planets while being in different phases of their elliptical trajectory around the sun, i.e., while being close to the sun, while being far off the sun and while being in an in-between position of their trajectory chart. These relative positions of any star and/or planet are supposed to make varying differences in the cosmic radiation reflected by it. Ancient astrologers developed nakshatra shastra through their interpretations of these varying differences in the cosmic rays of the stars and other planets as causing varying influences on human life.

It is said that some findings of the ancient rishis about the Sun, Moon, Jupiter and Mars, as elucidated in the Vedic literature, are quite similar to the findings of modern astronomy. Further, it is scientifically established that varying intensities of sunshine and other radiations from the sun, e.g., UV rays, during different time periods of the year in different places do bring different influences on human life, such as in affecting energy vigor, health, mood, happiness, etc. However, can such radiations cause windfall gain or sudden big loss to some persons without any visible causation is a big question. Though such cases are often seen to happen around us, these may as well be due to the unpredictable improbable chance factor as mentioned earlier. Nevertheless, more comprehensive scientific investigations are required to study the properties of cosmic radiations of various stars and planets in different phases of their trajectory before accepting or refuting their influences on human life on earth. Till then, the astrological beliefs will very much remain a part of even modern living, and much more in the traditional living of the religion.

CHAPTER

SPECIAL FEATURES OF THE RELIGION 04

As described in section 1.3.2, the vision of ancient rishis envisaged the protection of social ambiance as well as natural environment. Therefore, the rites and customs of the religion were developed in consonance with this vision. These rites and customs of the religion, practiced over generations, made a significant impact on both the natural environment and the social milieu over several millenniums until the recent times of modern science vision. These impacts became the special features of the religion and are described as follows.

4.1 PROTECTION OF NATURE

Protection of nature is the hallmark of the religion, which is clearly visible in the rituals and customs of the Vedic Sanatan religion. The ancient rishis gratefully realized the providence of nature in terms of food, fuel, fodder, fiber, timber, medicines, minerals and various other types of energy. Above all, they savored the peace and pleasure obtained in watching and enjoying the vast expanse of nature in different types of land masses like hills and plains, water bodies like rivers, lakes and sea, clouds and rains, sunshine and other cosmic exhibits, various plants, trees, forests and meadows, etc. Modern science, in terms of tedious jargons, symbols and equations was not known in those days, but the ancient rishis developed their own simple ancient science of realization and wisdom, and used it for protecting and preserving nature. They realized that with a growth in population and developmental activities, human greed would not be limited to any sensible boundary, and would soon destroy and degrade various elements of nature for their personal advantage. Hence, they found wisdom in the conceptualization of the various elements of nature as deities and developed several customary and religious rituals for their reverence and worship. In this way, they enlarged the domain of the religion from exclusive theology to nature protectionism.

Thus, earth, water, air, fire, plants and trees, and also the sun, moon, and other planets and sky all were treated as deities and worshipped on different festive and/or religious occasions as already described in section 3.2.1 and also at other places in that chapter. The ancient rishis knew that once people regarded the elements of nature as deities and revered and worshiped them, then no individual or group would be able to harm, spoil or pollute these elements due to intense social and religious pressure for the protection of these elements of nature. This way, a psychological barrier was created against possible harm or destruction of nature and its elements. To create this psychological barrier, some simple socio-religious reforms were initiated. First, the conservation of natural resources for survival was thoroughly impressed upon the minds of the people, and this was easily done by making the elements of nature deities to be revered and worshiped in all socio-religious ceremonies. Second, the habit of use, repair and reuse of resources was inculcated as the general practice in daily life as well as in special ceremonies in order to check wastage of the natural resources. In other words, this meant simple living and shunning all ostentatious shows by the masses. Third, this also necessitated punishment and a social boycott of those people unnecessarily resorting to undue harm and wastage of natural resources. In this way, the whole society, from children to grownups, was infused with the ideas of simple living and natural resource conservation and protection.

This has served as the best example of generating social awareness and pressure along with positive achievements in environmental protection in the past, which no other religion or country or institution has so far been able to achieve. In current times, only conferences, speeches and writings are done to represent the individual, social and international concern for the conservation and protection of the environment, which continues to degrade further with every passing year. Yet some scientists and rationalists are crying at the rituals and worship of the Vedic Sanatan religion as unscientific and orthodox, relating to tribal culture. In fact, they need to develop an unbiased vision and review of their opinion in view of the recent observations on the severe environmental degradation and pollution that is arising due to modern scientific and technological developments, and the much-hyped modern civilized culture, which, in fact, is worse than tribalism. In this regard, the practices and rituals of the Vedic Sanatan religion reflect the highest level of civilization and wisdom to have protected the environment for several millenniums—till the medieval period—despite high growth and development, which tempted other countries to invade this country for loot. Ignoring all these facts shows the blind-eye and closed-minded attitude of the snob critics.

Despite the great hue and cry over the past several decades at all levels, no worthwhile progress is visible in initiating meaningful actions for reducing pollution and environmental degradation. In fact, modern scientists, technocrats and bureaucrats while holding meetings and conferences on environment protection themselves substantially add up their carbon footprint through air-conditioned travel, stay and meeting rooms without any real outcome. A tremendous amount of money is being spent in various countries as well as at international levels, creating various paraphernalia in the name of environmental protection, but very little is visible in this regard. Furthermore, in the name of growth and development, very appealing speeches, write-ups and attractive advertisements are being made, which promote modern living based on a luxurious lifestyle and use and throw technology. Then, how would natural resource conservation and protection be initiated when a luxurious lifestyle and use and throw technology are responsible for environmental degradation? All this is happening because of a deterioration in the philosophical base of the religion's rites and customs due to the rush for modernity all around. Only simple living and reverence for all the elements of the natural environment, as advocated in the Vedic Sanatan religion, can check further degradation and also help in the restoration of the environment. In fact, all the units of the United Nations and its member countries should follow this dictum of the religion if they really have any concern for the environment and sustainability of good living on the earth in the long term. Growth and development are the secondary issues to be resolved by the appropriate technologies as done in ancient India.

The discoveries of modern science need to be reinterpreted in the background of degenerations in nature and society as against its present interpretations for commercial gains and growth. This will help in the development of appropriate technologies for social well-being as well as the protection of nature. Presently, modern technologies are fast-changing only to meet the market (commercial) sustainability and aggressive growth. Fast technological changes do not allow full plant depreciation and recovery of finance. This leads to an undue wastage of blocked natural resources and unpaid public/bank loans. Natural growth and simple living of the ancient model save both natural resources and the social milieu. Simple living does not mean living an ascetic life, it only means an austere living by reducing wastage of scarce resources in unnecessary showbiz and ostentations. Austerity dictum is to conserve the scarce and splurge the abundance.

4.2 ENERGY CONSERVATION

Energy conservation is another important element implicit in the set of tenets and practices of the Vedic Sanatan religion. Ancient thinkers had visualized that energy needs would increase many folds with the growth in population and developmental activities. Then forests would become the first victims to provide timber and fuel to meet the rising energy needs. The next in line would be the water bodies like ponds, lakes and rivers to provide water for the growing population and developmental activities. Both these elements of nature would be highly exploited. This would disturb and gradually destroy the local ecosystem comprising land, water and air, which would affect agriculture and animal production as also the lives of all living beings. Thus, they realized the rising need for energy and made energy conservation an important consideration while developing religious practices as well as development planning. This was achieved through the introduction of the following three components in the strategy for growth and development. Monitoring of growth and development was largely the responsibility of kings and courtiers. But some rishi known as RAJARSHI, who used to live in the kingdom as a courtier and was called the RAJGURU, used to give advice and guidance on growth and development activities too. These RAJARSHI used to consult the MAHARSHI who lived in forests and/or banks of some river and devoted themselves to yoga, meditation, theology and study of the nature and its phenomena. In this manner, the religion made a significant contribution to the conservation of energy by devising the following three components of the strategy for growth and development process.

The first component of the strategy was to promote industrial development only in limited basic fields such as textiles, mining and metallurgy, constructions, weaponry and tools manufacture. These basic fields were primarily labor intensive and most essential for accelerating the development process further. Mostly human and animal labor force was used for draught power as both these energy resources were easily available as well as reproducible. So, there were negligible or fewer inventions in labor-saving devices. Textiles were needed by everyone for social modesty as also for protection from climatic variations, which constituted the basic need after food. Mining and metallurgy were also necessary for the production of metals required for making tools and equipment needed for other developmental activities as also for making weapons for protection. Architecture was promoted for undertaking occasional large construction works like temples and palaces, which used to deploy a large force of artisans and casual workers in times of natural catastrophes to alleviate the suffering of the masses by providing some income and employment during lean periods. The ancient achievements in these fields, especially in textiles, metallurgy and architecture, along with those in spices production, medicines (Ayurvedic), mathematics and astronomy, won laurels for the country the world over. In addition, these achievements created so much wealth in the country, which later tempted several foreign invaders like Alexander from Greece in 326 BCE to several Tatars, Mongols, Mughals, and finally the Portuguese and British in the later periods for loot and plunder.

The second component of the strategy was to promote an austere lifestyle among the common people. There were three lifestyles prevalent in those days. One was ascetic living with a bare minimum for subsistence as followed by rishis and saints who generally lived in high hills or on the banks of rivers. They were mostly engaged in spirituality and the study of nature, and wandered in different places to discover knowledge about nature and its various elements. Second was austere living with essentials for a simple livable life, which was followed by the common people. They generally followed a dwelled life, engaged with their avocations and devoted their leisure time to religious practices that taught and inculcated the value of austere living among them. Austere living means avoiding wastage of income and scarce resources in ostentatious activities. Third was aristocratic living with luxuries as done by the kings and noble persons who were only a few and mostly lived in cities. These lifestyles, particularly the austere living by the masses, did not generate heavy demand for energy. The austere living by the masses, as promoted by the religion, was prevalent over several millenniums until the last and 20th century. In the 20th century, the race for modern technology led to growth and development initiated by democratic governance for raising the living standards of people as well as corporate industrialization, promoting luxuries through massive advertisements, have lured people, including the common man, to adopt modern luxurious living and shun the age-old simple austere lifestyle. This has now raised the energy demand tremendously.

The third component of the energy conservation strategy was the promotion of vegetarianism. Earlier all humans were carnivorous, hunting and killing animals for food. The advent of agriculture greatly opened the scope for herbivorous living. The religious belief that the same ISHWARA lives in all living beings in a subtle form, developed a feeling among most of the people to avoid killing animals for food. So, 'why kill a life for one's own food?' became a civilized dictum among most of the people following the religion. Furthermore, the ancient thinkers also discovered that an animal meat diet was more energy-consuming than a vegetarian diet because killing forest animals required more energy and time. Also, raising farm animals for meat required even more energy: first in growing food for farm animals, then in killing farm animals and processing the meat as food for human consumption. So, they thought that directly eating the farm-grown grains and vegetables would be the most energy-conserving. Thus, the concept of vegetarianism was evolved and promoted for energy conservation. Even those people who occasionally preferred eating meat as non-vegetarian food did not generally eat meat as a staple diet but took meat only as a supplement to lentils and vegetables; food grains were their staple food.

All the above three approaches for energy conservation worked quite well until recent times when science and technological developments and rapid industrialization became widely adopted. These changes have greatly reduced the real religious fervor on one hand, and have tremendously raised the craving for a new modern lifestyle on the other hand. As a result, the lifestyle of many people has drastically changed from the age-old simple living to a modern luxurious living like that of western countries. This is now leading to an enormous increase in energy demand, almost to the level of becoming an energy crisis. Much of modern technology is quite wasteful on both material and energy fronts as it is based on a linear progression of use—throw and build further—and not on the cyclical progression of use and reuse. The dictum of the modern technology-based corporate culture is to care only for the present time and the individual firm and its clientele, and not for the future of the society. The ancient and medieval technologies employed a more sustainable cyclical progression of use and reuse of material and energy sources, thereby, caring for the posterity as well. This feeling for the posterity kept the social institutions of family, relatives and social groups active and the social environment maintained. The energy-saving cyclical progression of use and reuse saved the natural resources and the environment from over-exploitation and degeneration. Thus, energy saving became a special feature of the religion.

4.3 LIBERTY OF BELIEF

The main doctrine of the religion states that BRAHMAN is not just matter but also spirit. It is the spirit that is life, which thinks, feels and observes, and is one and the same in everybody and everything. Spirit has three qualities of truth, consciousness and bliss (for details see section 2.2.1). Further, the functioning of the mind is also governed by conscience and consciousness, and not simply by the anatomy and physiology of the brain. Therefore, if some person is unable to grasp the truth about the BRAHMAN and thinks contrary about the religion because of some fraudulent knowledge, logic and realization, then the spirit of that person would not achieve the qualities of truth, consciousness and bliss in believing and following the Vedic Sanatan religion. Such a person would more likely debase the religion, and also despise and deter other believers of the religion. Ancient theologians thought that such persons would deteriorate not only the social milieu but also the religious fervor by not following the rituals and customs devised for protecting the natural environment that would soon start degrading. The philosophy of ancient theologians was to make the religion a realization, a way of life for the people and not an external imposition. Therefore, they did not put any restraint on believers of the religion, and such persons who thought contrary to the religion were freely allowed to change their religion or become atheist and/or heterodox. In fact, it did happen around 500 BCE, after the emergence of some new religious thoughts of Buddhism, Jainism and others. Many people then changed to other religions without any religious or social stigma, and this is still continuing even in the present times.

Thus, liberty of belief is another important feature of the Vedic Sanatan religion. The religion is passed on to the next generation in the family through various SAMSKARAS and the associated worship ceremonies, in which the child is made to participate and learn about the religion. However, when he grows up, the individual enjoys the freedom of belief and continuance in the religion or switches over to another faith and religion. Over time, many offshoots of the religion have emerged, the most prominent being Buddhism, Jainism, Sikhism, and ARYA SAMAJ, which all together along with the Vedic Sanatan religion are referred to as various faiths of HINDU religion the world over. There is no social stigma in being an atheist or deist or in adopting a particular faith of the Hindu religion or even another religion. Religion is a matter of belief. So, by adopting a religion, the person belongs to a religion and not vice-versa. This makes the Vedic Sanatan believer a passive follower of the religion and its practices. Thus, they do not preach, promote and protect the religion. The Vedic Sanatan religion does not preach bigotry nor react to blasphemy. There have been so many instances of foreign invasions and loot of wealth, destruction of temples and ancient manuscripts. The people calmly prayed to ISHWARA with full faith and trust, and rebuilt the wealth and temples. This is the concept of passive followers of religion as against the concept of active and aggressive followers of religion, in which people promote and protect their religion.

There is a celebrated example of the king ASHOK who after winning the battle of the KALINGA dynasty in 261 BCE felt aghast seeing the destructions caused by the war. So, as a repentance, he changed his religion to become a Buddhist and worked for the spread of Buddhism in India and other neighboring countries. In recent times, many people of the Vedic Sanatan religion have changed to ARYA SAMAJ, Buddhism, Jainism and other sects of the Hindu religion as also to other religions. Even within the Vedic Sanatan religion, an individual has the freedom to choose any form of ISHWARA for belief and worship, i.e., NIRAKAR or SAKAR. Within the SAKAR form, several incarnations or avatars of ISHWARA exist such as Vishnu, Shiva and Brahma. The individual is free to worship any form or all of these. This resilience to change or shift in faith and worship and liberty of belief has made the religion eternal without bigotry and without waging any religious war within the religion or with other religions over the past more than two millenniums. This is excellence and not cowardice or orthodoxy. Only recently, a very small group of political fanatics have shown some incidence of bigotry and religious intolerance at the invocation by some other religious and political groups. But this has not been favored or encouraged by the masses of the Vedic Sanatan religion. In fact, such incidences of religious bigotry have found more prominence only in politics and media for creating sensationalism, mainly for political gain. But it has found no response from the masses in general.

CHAPTER

THE CROSSROAD 05

Having gone through all the observations, facts and analyses presented so far, where does one find oneself reached? Obviously at a crossroad with three options for further moves. One option is going ahead straight with full faith and trust in the religion, and leading a traditional life following all the rites and customs as being scientific and/or full of wisdom. Faith and trust in ISHWARA will provide contentment, peace and solace, and the path of DHARMA will guide towards a virtuous, compassionate and cohesive living. This will not harm the social milieu and the ecosystem of nature as both are well protected by the tenets, rites and customs of the religion. The second option is turning to the right direction with full faith and trust in the religion, but leading a somewhat modified traditional life in view of a science and technology-dependent education system and source of livelihood, and following the rites and customs as being scientific and/or full of wisdom and also willing to resolve orthodoxy wherever found in tenets and customs. The path of DHARMA will guide towards a virtuous, compassionate and cohesive living. But a somewhat modified life as an admix of traditional and modern lifestyle will require strong concern and commitment to protecting the social milieu and nature, which are likely to be harmed by some elements of modern living. The third option is turning to the left direction with full conviction that ISHWARA and religion along with its tenets and customs are all unscientific and orthodox concepts. This will lead to atheism and heterodoxy, and the adoption of the modern lifestyle of western countries that is fully dependent upon science and technology, ignoring everything else. This almost means following the CHARVAK philosophy to live in the present, not bother about the past and future; just eat, drink and be merry. This happy-go-lucky lifestyle will have no concern and care for the social milieu and the natural environment, both of which would more likely face severe deterioration in the long run because of the selfish living and indiscriminate use of natural resources to support the high consumption level. A civilization based on such a lack of concern for social and natural environment is likely to face an early extinction by some natural catastrophes like a severe deluge, earthquake, drought, etc., as happened to some ancient civilizations in Egypt, Mid-Asia and South America. Thus, given all these possibilities, which option to choose at the crossroad is a moot choice to be made. The following reasoning and response may help resolve the dilemma at an individual level. But at a larger societal level, it will depend upon collective foresight, wisdom and response.

There is no compulsion on anyone to believe in ISHWARA and the religion; it is a matter of individual choice. The world exists and will continue to exist with all kinds of beliefs and faiths such as theists, atheists, deists and agnostics, as it all depends upon one's self-awareness. The religion and its Dharma (duty), however, inspires and inculcates virtues of self-control, compassion and cohesion among the believers, about which modern science and technology per se do not care. Modern science has developed tremendously to be able to explain many curiosities about nature and the universe; has very well served to cause a technological revolution, serving people with more comfort and luxury in life. But it has not filled the vacuum created by the neglect of the religion and, thereby the debase of virtues like self-control, compassion and cohesion as revealed by history time and again. History is full of examples of those who waged full-scale wars on others out of their pride and power achieved through science and technology and neglected dictums of their religion. The celebrated examples of the two world wars, the nuclear holocaust and genocide in the 20th century provide full testimony to this assertion.

Wars were fought for ages all over the world on the whims and ambitions of kings. But the timespan of wars and loss of men, materials and money in the earlier traditional wars were very small as compared to that in the two famous world wars and several other modern science and technology-triggered wars of recent times. At least there was no damage to the social structure and natural resource base in the ancient and medieval period wars. But the modern wars were loaded with destructive explosive arsenals in huge amounts, which, in addition to killing people, severely polluted the natural resource base of land, water and air, thereby degrading the environment. Ironically, most of the modern wars were initiated in the name of peace and justice, both of which were the first casualties of these wars. With the religion being relegated as unscientific and orthodox in the pretext of modernity and scientific living, the power of the religious force in taming the wild human minds has been reduced greatly to become almost ineffective everywhere. This encouraged more individual freedom with a neglectful attitude towards others. As a result, the war mania, full of a superiority complex, has dominated the world scenario during the past two centuries.

Further, due to the reduced and ineffective force of the religion and the associated Dharma in the past century, the concepts of modest living, social cohesion and compassion became sidetracked, and the craze for modern luxurious living with individual pride and conceit was greatly encouraged by the developments in science and technology. This led to an individual's identity surpassing compassion and social cohesion, thereby debasing the social institutions of family, relatives, friends and society, ultimately causing severe degradation in the social environment. On the other hand, to meet the rising demand for comforts and luxuries, further developments in science and technology were promoted and deployed to cause faster planned economic growth. This led to the emergence of a new trend of growth mania, in addition to the already existing war mania. The countries, business houses and people themselves, all over the world, got fully engrossed in running the rat race for faster planned economic growth instead of slow natural economic growth. This trend in faster economic growth initiated by the developments in science and technology in the past century has led to severe degradation in the natural environment as well as in the social environment.

As explained in section 1.3.2, the ancient growth model in India was developed in harmony with nature. It generated passive slow natural growth, and not only protected both the social environment and the natural environment for millenniums but also led to tremendous material growth in the country, which tempted some other countries for invasion and looting during the last millennium. Does this indicate primitive growth and tribal living in ancient times? Only the general level of living was practiced to be simple and austere in order to reduce the overall energy demand, and save natural resources and the environment. But in present times, the aggressive and active growth model, though has led to a tremendous increase in the general level of living, but at the cost of degradations in the social ambiance and natural resources. The recent climate changes, now occurring due to environmental degradation, indicate nature's wrath and resistance to the current levels of human greed for economic growth. The ancient thinkers were apprehensive of such nature's wrath, to avoid which they practiced the non-resisting natural slow growth model.

Like the war mania overshadowing peace and justice as said earlier, the growth mania also overshadows the reality of happy well-being for the masses. Growth is planned for generating income and employment and raising the living standards of people. But growth requires energy from electricity for running factories and establishments, and also energy from diesel and petrol for transport of inputs and outputs in industries. About two-thirds of the electricity is generated by burning coal in thermal power plants. The smoke produced by burning coal and diesel is highly carcinogenic, leading to an increase in incidences of cancer, tuberculosis, asthma, and severe eye and nose allergies, all requiring highly sophisticated and costly medical care besides creating an unhealthy being. In addition, this leads to the depletion and degradation of the natural resource base of hydrocarbons and the other associated minerals, and also contributes to air pollution, global warming and climate change. Moreover, planned aggressive growth generally leads to higher corporate incomes and highly skilled job creation as compared to the trickle-down benefit effect of an increase in income and employment at the lower levels. Life has become more glamorous but serious morbidities and mental stress have also increased proportionally. All these adverse side effects overshadow the reality of the rise in living standards and the happy well-being of the masses.

So, the real issue is not whether ISHWARA exists or whether the religion is an unscientific and orthodox concept. Chapter 2 of the book fully elaborates that BRAHMAN or ISHWARA exists as an infinite formless energy, which in subtle quantum pervades everything everywhere all the time. The chapter also elaborates that the tenets, rites and customs of the religion inculcate the virtues of discipline, self-control, compassion and cohesion in the human mind, which otherwise may run amuck causing conflicts, wars and destruction to the natural resources. Therefore, the real issue is how to reduce the war mania as well as the growth mania. In other words, how to regulate the adverse effects of developments in science and technology to check further destruction in both the social environment and the natural environment? For several millenniums, till the medieval period, the religion helped regulate and control human greed and wildness through its tenets and socio-religious customs that inspire modest living, virtuousness, social cohesion, awe of ISHWARA, and love and care for various elements of nature and society.

But nowadays, the religion is relegated by the craze for modernity, which is adversely affecting the social fabric of family, relatives and other social groups as also degrading the natural resource base. The concern for the degeneration of the social environment is totally missing, not even being noticed at all. Only the concern for the degradation of the natural environment is visible and being debated. But it is also casually left to the hope of some new technology developments to resolve the problem. Knowing fully well that every new technological solution brings in new issues and problems after some time, technology cannot be treated as a panacea for all ills. The rat race for technology and economic growth is so mesmerizing that people at all levels are adopting a blind-eye and closed-minded attitude. The problems are getting aggravated and the people are busy finding technological solutions instead of focusing on their own actions in reducing levels of luxurious living, energy consumption and indiscriminate use of the natural resources.

Therefore, people themselves have to think about their choice and preference for modernity along with the concern and care needed for preserving society and nature. There are three types of concerns and cares. One, the realized concern and care, which entails some foresight and sacrifice. Second, the obligatory concern and care, which entails belief in tradition and its follow-up. Third, the legalized concern and care, which entails compliance with legal decree. The best, though most difficult, is the realized concern and care, which is based on self-realization of the need for it and leads to some definite achievement. But it does involve some sacrifice on one's part, especially some modifications in lifestyle. Next is obligatory concern and care, which is based on the sense of fulfilling obligations built in the traditional lifestyle. This is mostly seen in practice by some people as it easily fits in while following the tradition without any resentment and sacrifice. The third one of legalized concern and care is based on the state decree forcing people to follow some rules in order to provide some care. Such rules are resented by some, if not by all, and so these usually remain uncared for follow up until vigorously enforced. Therefore, the readiness to offer a particular type of concern and care may help decide the awareness and willingness for the cause of the society and environment, and thereby selection of one out of the three options available at the crossroad mentioned in the beginning.

People must ask themselves if they can live without the attractive and serene views of rivers, lakes, seas, mountains and valleys. If they can really live so, then why do they occasionally go on holiday to visit these places? Similarly, they must also ask themselves if they can feel happy and enjoy their achievements and fancies without sharing these with their family, friends and others in the society. If they can really feel happy and enjoy so, then will they not become like Robinson Crusoe on a virgin island or robots in themselves? If they find the answer as 'NO' to these questions, then they must get themselves ready for realized care or at least obligatory care, requiring some sacrifice in their lifestyle by reducing energy consumption in the name of preserving the natural environment and also building family communion to preserve the social milieu. Then they can make a holiday trip to any natural and scenic place to appreciate their own role in preserving nature. As for preserving the social ambiance, start mixing and rejoicing with the family, friends and relatives by actual participation in family functions and festivals without any individual pride and prejudice.

Therefore, if family, friends and society as also the diversity in the environment hold any importance, then either go straight or turn to the right at the crossroad mentioned in the beginning. Going straight will require only obligatory care because following the religion as such does no harm to society and the environment. But turning to the right will require realized care for both the society and the environment in terms of some sacrifices to be made by some modifications in the modern lifestyle while faithfully following the religion. The modifications in modern lifestyle require significant reductions in energy consumption, which means a significant curtail in the use of electricity, diesel and petrol as also reducing other wastefulness of resources such as water, paper, plastics, etc. Likewise, shunning use and throw practices, and craze for the latest models of all types of modern gadgets is also required because it will not only reduce the wasteful use of several resources to be saved for posterity but also decrease waste disposal problems. But this would be possible only when there is realized concern and care for a clean environment and livable society. All this would mean creating real awareness about the self, the society and the environment.

In the end, it is worthwhile to mention that everything being said and done these days in the name of the Vedic Sanatan religion is not necessarily all scientific and/or full of wisdom content. While some may exhibit scientific connotations and/or wisdom content, others may just be a deception on scientific and religious interpretations. There may be many people who may have their own interpretations, as being different from those presented in this book. Personal interpretations are influenced by emotion, devotion, education and profession, and their spectrum varies widely with time among various individuals. There are some priests who make their own interpretations to propagate blind faith in the name of ISHWARA and conduct religion's rites, customs and related ceremonies, befooling the gullible people to plunder money from them. In ancient days, the priests were generally guided by their devotion and education, which inculcated among them the virtue of simple austere living with contentment. In present times, they are exposed to the demonstration effect, i.e., what is happening around in the neighborhood. So, some of them get tempted to make more money through plunder and befooling the client into conducting religious rites and customs by imposing their own interpretations and even devising some tantrum and black magic. Thus, they are debasing the Vedic Sanatan religion and cheating the gullible people. This needs to be checked. Therefore, all religious training institutions, religious congregations, temples and spiritual celebrities should attempt to educate the people on the methods deployed by fraudulent priests.

It may be worthwhile to prepare books in regional languages, detailing procedures for the conduct of the rites and customs of the Vedic Sanatan religion so that people may understand and verify the manner of conduct of any rite or custom by the priest and protest if not done properly. Presently, most people are unaware of these details in the absence of such books. This work may be entrusted to a consortium of learned saints and priests, collectively invoked by renowned temples and religious institutions through congregation on the religion. This consortium after 'shashtrarth' may finalize the content of the book in Sanskrit/English language, which may then be translated into regional languages for publication by some regional religious institutions and temples that have resources to spare. These books will help integration of the believers of the religion across different languages and regions through common practices for conducting the rites and customs of the religion. Such books will also help check the improper practices of the fraudster priests as people will be equipped with knowledge about these practices.

REFERENCES

1. Central Hindu College, Benares, India (1916), SANATAN DHARMA, an elementary textbook of HINDU RELIGION AND ETHICS, published by the Board of Trustees, Central Hindu College, Benares, printed by TARA printing works, Benares, digitized for Microsoft Corporation by the Internet Archive in 2007 from the University of California Libraries, printed copy available on 'amazon.in'.
2. Dayanand Saraswati (2005), Satyarth Prakash (Hindi), 2021 edition, published by KIRAN publication, Delhi – 110092, printed by Shiv Shakti printers, Delhi – 110032, available on 'amazon.in'.
3. Hindu Janajagruti Samiti (2002), Great Indian Hindu Sages who revolutionized the field of science, https://www.hindujagruti.org.
4. Mani Bhaumic (2021), Indic Wisdom Meets QUANTUM PHYSICS, Times of India, February 06, 2021, New Delhi/Pune.
5. Mathur P.C. (2016), Ignorance of the Learned: Science of Religion and Religion of Science, Notion Press, Chennai – 600031.
6. Pattanaik Devdatta (2006), MYTH = MYTHYA, Decoding Hindu Mythology, Penguin Random House India Limited, Gurgaon – 122002.
7. Srinivasan Chakrapani (2022), Roots of Modern Science in Ancient Scriptures, Readers' Blog, June 11, 2022, https:// timesofindia.indiatimes.com.
8. Tong David (2017), Quantum Fields: The Real Building Blocks of the Universe, Lecture delivered in the Royal Institution, London, U.K., YouTube Videos pdf 2021.
9. Yuval Noah Harari (2014), Sapiens, A Brief History of Humankind, Penguin Random House, U.K., Vintage Books, London, U.K.

APPENDIX

Appendix Table: Contributions of the ancient Indian sages/rishis in the field of science.

Sl. No.	Name of Sage/Rishi (Period)	Scientific Knowledge Developed
1	KAPIL MUNI (3000 BCE)	Founder of Sankhya philosophy (Tatva darshan), delving into nature and the principles of the ultimate soul (Purusha), primal matter (Prakruti) and creation; developed the concept of transformation of energy; asserted that Prakruti, with the inspiration of Purusha, is the mother of cosmic creation and all energies. Recognized as the Father of Cosmology.
2	BHASKARACHARYA (1114-1183 BCE)	Algebra, Arithmetic and Geometry; two mathematical works "Bijaganita" and "Lilavati" have been translated into several languages; another treatise "Siddhant Shiromani" described planetary positions, eclipses and cosmography; described that objects fall on earth due to force of attraction; earth, planets, moon, and sun are held in orbit due to this force of attraction.
3	BHARADWAJ (800 BCE)	Aviation technology; wrote "Yantra Sarvasva" covering discoveries in aviation science, space science and flying machines; described three types of flying machines: one flying from one place to another on earth, second for travels from one planet to another, and third for travels from one universe to another.
4	KANAD (600 BCE)	Atomic Theory and philosophy; founder of "Vaisheshik Darshan", one of the six principal philosophies of India; pioneer expounder of realism, the law of causation and atomic theory; said that every object of creation is made of atoms; also described the dimension and motion of atoms and their chemical reactions with each other.
5	SUSHRUT (600 BCE)	Surgery; text on "Sushrut Samhita" is an encyclopedia of surgery; recognized as the Father of Plastic Surgery and the science of anesthesia; used 125 types of surgical instruments.

6	CHARAK (600 BCE)	Ayurvedic medicine; revealed facts on human anatomy, embryology, pharmacology, blood circulation, and diseases like diabetes, tuberculosis, heart problems, etc.; textual "Charak Samhita" described the medicinal qualities and functions of 100,000 herbal plants; emphasized the influence of diet and activity on mind and body.
7	VARAHMIHIR (499-587 BCE)	Astronomy; textual contribution "Panchsiddhant" holds a prominent place in astronomy; described that the moon and planets are lustrous not because of their own light but due to sunlight; In other texts "Bruhad Samhita" and "Bruhad Jatak" revealed his discoveries in the fields of geography, constellation science, botany and animal sciences.
8	ARYABHATT (476 BCE)	Mathematics and astronomy; wrote "Aryabhattam" in 499 BCE a treatise on mathematics and astronomy; proclaimed that the earth is round, rotates on its axis, orbits the sun and is suspended in space; the contribution of zero, calculation of Pi up to four decimal places, and the sine table in trigonometry were colossus contributions.
9	PATANJALI (200 BCE)	Science of Yoga; prescribed the control of prana (life breath) as the means to control the body, mind and soul for good health and inner happiness; developed 84 yogic postures/asanas to enhance the efficiency of the respiratory, circulatory, nervous, digestive and endocrine systems and many other organs of the body.
10	NAGARJUNA (100 BCE)	Chemistry and metallurgy; "Ras Ratnagar" and "Rashrudaya" and "Rasendramangal" are textual contributions in chemistry; "Yogasar" and "Arogyamanjari" are textual contributions in curative medicine.

Source: Hindu Janajagruti Samiti (2012), Great Indian Hindu Sages who revolutionized the field of science, https://www.hindujagruti.org

INDEX

www.ingramcontent.com/pod-product-compliance
Lightning Source LLC
LaVergne TN
LVHW091056150826
845673LV00002B/602

* 9 7 9 8 8 9 2 3 3 4 2 9 7 *